Angels
For Beginners

About the Author

Richard Webster is the author of more than fifty titles with Llewellyn, and he is one of New Zealand's most prolific writers. His best-selling books include *Face Reading Quick & Easy*, *Spirit Guides and Angel Guardians*, *Miracles*, and a series of books on feng shui. MagicNZ presented him with a Lifetime Achievement Award for "excellence in writing magical literature" in 2008. His book *Spirit and Dream Animals* received a COVR Award in 2012. In 2013, Richard was made a Grand Master of Magic by the magicians of New Zealand. He has appeared on numerous TV shows including *Hard Copy* and *20/20*. His books have been translated into thirty-one languages.

Angels

For Beginners

Understand & Connect
with Divine Guides & Guardians

Richard Webster

Llewellyn Publications
Woodbury, Minnesota

FIRST EDITION
First Printing, 2017

Cover art: SuperStock/900-7560: The Guardian Angel/©Wilhelm Von Kaulbach
Cover design: Lisa Novak

Llewellyn Publications is a registered trademark of Llewellyn Worldwide Ltd.

Library of Congress Cataloging-in-Publication Data

Names: Webster, Richard, author.
Title: Angels for beginners : understand & connect with divine guides &
    guardians / Richard Webster.
Description: Woodbury : Llewellyn Worldwide, Ltd, 2017. | Includes
    bibliographical references.
Identifiers: LCCN 2016048905 (print) | LCCN 2017001688 (ebook) | ISBN
    9780738751153 | ISBN 9780738752112 (ebook)
Subjects: LCSH: Angels. | Abrahamic religions.
Classification: LCC BL477 .W4248 2017 (print) | LCC BL477 (ebook) | DDC
    202/.15—dc23
LC record available at https://lccn.loc.gov/2016048905

Llewellyn Publications
A Division of Llewellyn Worldwide Ltd.
2143 Wooddale Drive
Woodbury, MN 55125-2989
www.llewellyn.com

Printed in the United States of America

Other Books by Richard Webster

Astral Travel for Beginners
Aura Reading for Beginners
Body Language Quick & Easy
Candle Magic for Beginners
Color Magic for Beginners
Creative Visualization for Beginners
Dowsing for Beginners
The Encyclopedia of Superstitions
Face Reading Quick & Easy
Feng Shui for Beginners
Flower and Tree Magic
Gabriel
Geomancy for Beginners
Is Your Pet Psychic?
Living in Your Soul's Light
Magical Symbols of Love & Romance
Michael
Miracles
Palm Reading for Beginners
Pendulum Magic for Beginners
Practical Guide to Past-Life Memories
Praying with Angels
Psychic Protection for Beginners
Raphael
Rituals for Beginners
Soul Mates
Spirit & Dream Animals
Spirit Guides & Angel Guardians
Uriel
Write Your Own Magic

Dedication

For Kiera, our littlest angel

contents

Five

The Specialist Angels 99

Six

How to Communicate with Angels II9

Seven

Working with Angels I47

Eight

Angelic Visitations I75

Conclusion I89

Appendix A:

Angels in Art, Literature, and Music I89

Appendix B:

Angels for Different Purposes 209

References 2I3

I didn't see my grandmother often when I was growing up, as she lived almost a thousand miles away. Consequently, when she came to visit, she often stayed for a few weeks. She was a stern, forbidding woman, but I remember a number of tender moments. One of these was her sitting on my bed when I was about five or six, teaching me children's prayers and traditional rhymes. The one I remember best is this familiar prayer:

> *Matthew, Mark, Luke, and John,*
> *Bless the bed that I lie on.*
> *Four angels to my bed,*
> *Four angels round my head.*

> *One to watch, and one to pray,*
> *And two to bear my soul away.*

Fortunately, I didn't learn what the final line meant until many years later. This must have been the first time I heard about angels.

I attended a church school, and the only thing I learned about angels there was that they were "God's helpers" who conveyed messages to and from God. Catholic friends who lived nearby occasionally mentioned their guardian angels. When I asked the chaplain at my school a question about them, he told me that children who went to the Catholic school down the road had guardian angels, but we didn't need them. I was in my twenties when I discovered that I not only had a guardian angel but also needed him. It took me many years to learn that there was much more to angels than that.

Other people discover angels when they see one for the first time or sense an angelic presence. A friend of mine lived in Japan for several years. One night he woke up and saw a small winged angel wearing a kimono. He wasn't religious and was surprised to see an angel.

My next-door neighbor has seen angels on several different occasions. She sees them as glowing, golden balls of light. She finds it comforting to see them, as they always appear at times when she needs help or has an important decision to make.

Many people experience the presence of an angel but don't realize it until later. A good example is an elderly woman who was traveling to see her grandchildren who lived a hundred miles away. It was winter, and she was finding it difficult to drive along snow-covered country roads. She found a place to park her car off the road and decided to wait until conditions improved before continuing on to her destination. She locked all the doors, lay down on the back seat, and tried to get to sleep. After about thirty minutes, she heard a gentle, but persistent, tapping on the windshield. She told me she was curious, and, unusual for her, unafraid. She opened the window slightly and called out to whoever or whatever it was.

A young man, dressed immaculately in a business suit, came up to the window and said hello to her. He said that he lived in a nearby farm house and had seen her park her car. As it was snowing and the temperature was dropping, he'd come to see if he could offer any help.

"You can stay at our farm overnight if you wish," he said. "Or I could drive your car to your grandchildren's home."

The woman was so surprised that it wasn't until much later that she thought how strange it was that someone who lived on a farm was wearing business clothes or that he knew she was driving to see her grandchildren.

"I really want to get to my daughter's home," she said.

The man seemed so honest and sincere that she allowed him into the car, and he drove her the rest of the way. Halfway there, she asked him how he'd get back to his farm. The man smiled and said, "Someone's waiting to drive me back." Again, these surprising words seemed perfectly normal to the tired and confused woman.

When they reached her destination, the young man carried her luggage up to the front door, handed her the car keys, and turned to walk away.

"Thank you," the woman said. "Please tell me your name."

The man smiled, walked to the end of the driveway, and disappeared. As she knocked on her daughter's front door, she felt that it must have been a hallucination and that she'd actually driven all the way herself. This thought was completely dispelled when her grandchildren opened the door and asked who the man was that they'd seen carrying her bags to the front door. This woman now believes in angels, as she's totally convinced that the young man who helped her was, in fact, an angel.

Some people receive regular messages from angels. These usually appear as thoughts in their minds, although some people hear the messages as if someone was speaking to them. One woman I met told me that she'd been receiving, and acting upon, angelic messages for more than forty years.

On one occasion, she was traveling by bus and was getting ready to get off at the next stop. She received a thought telling her to stay on the bus. She was surprised but, as she trusted her guardian angel, stayed where she was. Two stops later, a man came on board and sat down beside her. He had a pleasant smile, and before long they were chatting to each other as if they'd been friends for years. When he reached his destination, he asked her if she'd like to have a cup of coffee with him. She agreed. As she got off the bus, she thought how out of character this was. However, she felt comfortable with the man, and they enjoyed a pleasant conversation as they sipped their coffees. When they finished, they exchanged phone numbers. The relationship blossomed, and just over two years later, they married. If this woman hadn't listened to her guardian angel, the chances are that she would never have met her future husband.

A number of people have experienced being touched by an angel. A man I know was visiting his wife in the hospital. She was terminally ill with cancer and declining quickly. As he sat beside her bed trying to contain his tears, he felt a gentle touch on his cheek. The knowledge that he was surrounded by angels provided comfort and told him that he and his wife would meet again and continue their relationship in the afterlife.

A few people have told me that they've experienced angel wings wrapped around them at times when they've needed protection. Although they haven't been able to see the angel, they've gained comfort and strength from the knowledge that they are being helped by angels when they really need it.

From the dawn of civilization, people have believed that dreams are a highly effective way for divine beings to send messages to people. When we're dreaming, our minds are more receptive to the imagery and symbolism in the messages that come from the divine. Over the years, many people have told me about their experiences with angels in their dreams. This isn't surprising, because when we're asleep, we temporarily let go of our rational left brain and are able to access our subconscious minds and become aware of messages from the divine.

Many people receive signs of an angelic presence. Some people notice white feathers or experience a beautiful, delicate floral scent that tells them angels are present. Others hear angelic music, as if a magnificent choir was singing solely for them. Unexplained sparkles of light can be a sign of angels. Some people see angels in cloud formations, while others experience a strong feeling that they're in the company of angels.

It seems that angels can make their presence known in many different ways that are personal to each individual.

It makes no difference how you experience angels. The important part is to welcome them into your life, and to allow them to help you. This book will help you increase your knowledge of angels and hopefully enable you to experience them for yourself.

The first chapter discusses angels: what they are, what they look like, and what they do. The second chapter looks at the hierarchy of angels, which explains how the angels are divided up into different groups. In many ways it's like a government department, with a number of different rankings. Chapter 3 discusses guardian angels. We all have a special angel who protects, helps, and guides us from the moment we're born. This chapter will help you communicate with your guardian angel and strengthen the connection you have with him. Chapter 4 looks at the archangels, focusing mainly on "the big four" of Michael, Gabriel, Raphael, and Uriel. Chapter 5 looks at some of the specialist angels, such as the angels of healing and the angels of abundance. These particular angels are there to provide you with help in special situations. Chapter 6 covers how to communicate with angels. Chapter 7 covers how to work with the angelic realms. A number of rituals are included to help you do this. Chapter 8 covers angelic visitations throughout history and discusses a number of specific instances of angelic communication. Appendix A looks at the role of angels in art, literature, and music. Appendix B contains a list of problems and concerns and suggests specific angels who can help resolve them. All biblical quotations come from the King James Version of the Bible. References in the text will include the chapter and verse numbers.

I hope this book will encourage you to look further into the world of angels and to make them an integral part of your life.

one

What Are Angels?

Dictionaries define angels as spiritual beings who attend to God and act as divine messengers. Almost all of the major religions accept the idea of angels acting as go-betweens between God and humanity. In fact, the word angel comes from the Greek word *angelos*, which means "messenger." In the Bible angels are described as "ministering spirits, sent forth to minister for them who shall be heirs of salvation" (Hebrews 1:14). Angels are servants of God who exist solely to carry out his will (Tobit 12:18). John of Damascus wrote this detailed account of what an angel is: "an intelligent essence, in perpetual motion, with free will, incorporeal, ministering to God, having obtained by grace an immortal nature: and the Creator alone knows the form and limitation of its essence" (John of Damascus [1988] 2009).

Saint Thomas Aquinas believed that angels were comprised of pure thought or intellect. They could assume physical bodies whenever they wanted to, but even these were comprised of pure thought. Meister Eckhart, the German theologian and philosopher, wrote, "That's all an Angel is; an idea of God" (von Hochheim 1998).

Although many people have tried, no one has been able to give a conclusive answer to the question "What are angels?" The general consensus seems to be that they are celestial beings of pure light who operate on a different vibrational frequency from us. This makes them invisible to human eyes. However, angels can change their vibrations whenever they wish. When they lower their vibrations to a human level, we can become aware of their presence and sometimes even see them. Angels protect and guide mankind and usually appear in extraordinary situations, such as when someone needs help, protection, or comfort. Although the traditional view of an angel is of a small cherub with wings, angels can change their shape and form whenever they wish. This means you might see an angel as a person, a butterfly or other winged figure, a rainbow, a bright light, or anything else. Angels are genderless and can appear in both male and female form. However, all the references to angels in the Bible appear to be masculine, rather than feminine. In the Jewish tradition, angels are considered masculine.

Angels can appear in any form they wish. In the Bible they always appear as male adults, but there are many reports of angels appearing as children, adolescents, and women.

This is because these people usually appear nonthreatening, and we're prepared to listen and communicate with them. People usually expect them to have wings, but this is rare when they choose to appear as human beings.

Saint Padre Pio always saw his guardian angel as a child. On one occasion he answered a knock at his door, and said, "Ah, it is you, my Little Angel. It is you, Little Boy" (Parente 1984, 28–29).

Angels are often portrayed as warriors in the endless battle against evil. This might be why they are usually depicted in male form. Because they are powerful, the first words an angel says to a human in the Bible are "Do not be afraid" (Daniel 8:17; Daniel 10:11; Matthew 28:5; Mark 16:6; Luke 1:12–13; Luke 2:9; Acts 10:4).

Some people claim that angel wings were created by artists to demonstrate the difference between angels and humans in their works of art. However, as far back as the book of Exodus, which was written in the sixth century BCE, there is mention of angels possessing wings. When God told Moses to build the Ark of the Covenant, he specifically told him to "make two cherubims of gold, of beaten work shalt thou make them, in the two ends of the mercy seat. And make one cherub on the one end, and the other cherub on the other end: even of the mercy seat shall ye make the cherubims on the two ends thereof. And the cherubims shall stretch forth their wings on high, covering the mercy seat with their wings, and their faces shall look one to another" (Exodus 25:18–20).

In the book of Jubilees, one of the apocryphal religious texts that was left out of the Bible, angels are said to have been created on the first day, after the heavens and earth but before the firmament. This means that angels were able to help God with his creation. However, traditional belief says that angels were created on the second day of Creation. No matter which day is correct, angels live in heaven with God. They are free of the emotions, such as anger and jealousy, that make people unhappy. This lack of negativity enables them to live in the presence of the divine, and enjoy being in God's presence.

Angels possess free will. Lucifer is the best-known example of this. He wasn't content to be one of the most important angels, and decided he wanted God's power. This led to the war in heaven, which Lucifer lost. He and his followers, said to be a third of all the angels, were expelled from heaven.

Other authorities believe that angels worship God unceasingly, twenty-four hours a day. As they don't need to sleep, they can keep worshiping and praising God constantly for all eternity.

No one knows how many angels there are, though the number is enormous. In Revelations 5:11, John describes how he "heard the voice of many angels round about the throne and the beasts and the elders: and the number of them was ten thousand times ten thousand, and thousands and thousands."

Angels through History

Belief in angels is extremely old. The oldest-known depiction of an angel is on a Sumerian stele that is six thousand years old. It shows a winged figure pouring the water of life into a cup belonging to a king (Roland 1999, 12). Five thousand years ago, the ancient Sumerians believed in divine messengers and guardian angels. These were called *anunnaki*, which means "creatures from the sky" (Garrett 2015, 64). Many of the Sumerian stone carvings of winged beings still exist today.

Twenty-five hundred years later, an angel called Vohu-Manah delivered God's message to a Persian mystic called Zoroaster, the founder of Zoroastrianism. This religion is still practiced today by a few hundred thousand people in Iran and western India. Zoroastianism had a huge influence on the beliefs of Judaism, Christianity, and Islam. In this religion, there are six archangels and a number of lesser angels, including guardian angels who look after the interests of one human being. These guardian angels are called *fravashi*.

The concept of guardian angels was also strong in ancient Mesopotamia, where people were "surrounded and protected by one or more supernatural beings charged with that specific function" (Oppenheim 1964, 199).

Judaism adopted angels as part of their belief system. This included the concept of archangels. In the Old Testament two archangels are mentioned by name: Michael and Gabriel. Two more, Raphael (in the book of Tobit) and Uriel (in the book of Esdras), appear in the apocryphal Old Testament.

It took until the eighth century CE before Christianity acknowledged the reality of angels. In 325 CE the First Ecumenical Council accepted the existence of angels. However, this was rescinded twenty years later when the Second Council concluded that belief in angels hindered people from worshipping Christ. Finally, in 787 CE, the Seventh Ecumenical Synod decided that the Christian Church believed angels were created to intercede between man and God.

Christianity created a bureaucracy of angels, listing them in ranks, similar to a business hierarchy. In the New Testament there is mention of thrones, dominions, virtues, powers, principalities, archangels, and angels. Two more, cherubims and seraphims, appear in the Old Testament, providing nine ranks of angels.

Saint Hildegard of Bingen, the German mystic, abbess, composer, and writer, believed that the hierarchy of angels was arranged in concentric circles that made it easier for each group to communicate with the others. She also believed in guardian angels, but felt they existed only to help people who feared and loved God (Hildegard 1985).

Saint Thomas Aquinas, the Italian philosopher, theologian, and jurist, wrote *Summa Theologica*, which explains how angels communicate, how they travel, and why they are essential for life on earth. He believed that angels were created from pure intellect but could use mental energy to create a physical form when required.

In the sixteenth century Dr. John Dee, the celebrated astrologer and occultist, and his scryer, Edward Kelley, claimed to have transcribed the secret language of angels. The perfect syntax and grammar, not to mention the beauty, of this Enochian language leave no doubt that they did communicate with the angelic kingdom.

In the nineteenth century, the Hermetic Order of the Golden Dawn adopted this language of the angels. This created a whole new interest in the subject, and the Enochian language is still being used in ceremonial magic today.

Emanuel Swedenborg, the eminent Swedish scientist and philosopher, is arguably considered the most famous person in the history of angelology. He regularly communicated with angels and wrote many books about his experiences. He claimed to have visited heaven and spoken with angels. He believed that as angels did not reflect the sun's rays, they were invisible to most people and could be seen only through intuition. Although he thought that few people could speak to angels directly, he felt everyone could benefit by learning more about them. He also believed that every angel had lived on earth as a human being before becoming an angel.

Swiss theologian Karl Barth believed that angels brought heaven to people on earth. When they speak to us, he said, we are actually hearing God. Likewise, when angels act, it is God acting. Karl Barth thought that angels were both above and below us. They were above us as they could watch God at work. However, they were also below us, as God's work was directed at humans, rather than the angelic kingdom. He wrote, "To deny the angels is to deny God himself" (Barth 1960, 486).

Angels in Christianity

Much of our knowledge about angels comes from the Christian tradition, though not all of the early Christian Fathers were prepared to accept them.

Christianity gradually adopted the concept of guardian angels, although there is disagreement about whether God provides everyone with an individual guardian angel. There are three passages in the Bible that appear to refer to guardian angels:

1. "For he shall give his angels charge over thee, to keep thee in all thy ways. They shall bear thee up in their

hands, lest thou dash thy foot against a stone" (Psalms 91:11–12).

2. Jesus, speaking about children, said, "In heaven their angels do always behold the face of my Father which is in heaven" (Matthew 18:10).

3. Acts 12 recounts how an angel rescued Peter from prison. The people at the home of Mary, mother of John the Baptist, declared, "It is his angel" (Acts 12:15).

According to the Bible, angels are highly intelligent beings who "know all things that are in the earth" (2 Samuel 14:20). They are possibly best known as being God's messengers. Angels have a strong sense of right and wrong, and when necessary serve as God's warriors. They provide help and protection for people who need it. One of the best known verses in the Bible about angels says, "For he shall give his angels charge over thee, to keep thee in all thy ways" (Psalms 91:11). Because angels are immortal, there is no need for them to reproduce. Consequently, they are genderless and can appear in any form they wish. They often appear as humans. Angels constantly attend the throne of God.

Angels in Judaism

In the Jewish tradition, angels are spiritual beings who possess no physical qualities. The wings and arms, mentioned in Jewish writings, are not meant to be interpreted literally, as they refer to the spiritual qualities of angels. The Hebrew word for angel is *malach*, which means messenger. Angels do not possess free will, and they are created to worship God and to be his messengers. Unlike the Christian tradition, Jewish angels are programmed to do specific tasks. Some angels are created to perform one particular task, and, once this task has been accomplished, the angel ceases to exist. Jewish angels sing and praise God at different times, taking turns to ensure God is worshipped twenty-four hours a day.

Jewish philosophers enjoy discussing whether the angels who appear in the Torah—the first five books of the Bible—were in physical form or were seen in a vision and appeared to be in a physical body.

Angels are not worshipped in the Jewish tradition. God makes all the decisions, and angels exist solely to carry out his instructions.

In the Jewish tradition, Michael is believed to be the guardian of the Israelites. He is compassionate and kind yet strong and powerful when necessary. He is the angel who is usually chosen to carry out God's instructions. Gabriel is the angel of strength and judgment. Raphael is the angel of healing, and Uriel encourages people to find, and stay on, the right path.

Angels in the Church of Latter-Day Saints

A momentous angelic encounter occurred in the United States on September 21, 1823. An angel called Moroni appeared to a young man called Joseph Smith and told him to go to a hill in New York state where he would find a number of gold plates that contained the book of Mormon. Moroni appeared to Joseph Smith three times during the night, and again the next day. Joseph Smith found the plates but was unable to remove them. Moroni appeared again and said it was too soon to retrieve the plates and translate them from Hebrew into English. Joseph waited patiently for four years. After he'd translated the plates, Moroni appeared again and took the plates back to heaven. By this time, Joseph had learned enough to start the Church of Jesus Christ of Latter-Day Saints. Today, a large statue of Moroni is on top of the Mormon Tabernacle in Salt Lake City.

Joseph Smith also claimed that certain gifted people can become angels after their death. Consequently, John the Baptist, now an angel, restored the Aaronic priesthood. In the same way, Peter, James, and John, former disciples but now angels, restored the Melchizedek priesthood. In this religion, all angels have either lived lives as human beings or will become humans at sometime in the future. Angels who possess a physical body have lived on earth as humans. Angels without a physical body have not yet lived lives as humans. In Mormonism, Adam, the first man, is believed to be Archangel Michael, and Noah is now Archangel Gabriel.

Mormons believe that angels are messengers of God. They look like human beings and do not have wings. They are not worshipped or venerated, as everything they do is under the direction of Jesus Christ. There are no guardian angels in the Mormon religion, but angels do pass on comfort, help, protection, and love to humans.

Angels in Islam

Angels play a major role in Islam, too. Belief in angels is one of the six articles of faith. In the Night Journey, one of the foundation stones of Islam, Djibril (the angel Gabriel, also known as Jibril, Jibra'il, and Gibrail in Islam) visited Muhammad in Mecca and flew with him to Jerusalem, where they spoke with Abraham, Moses, Jesus, John the Baptist, and other prophets. After this they climbed a ladder to heaven where Djibril took him to meet God. It was here that Muhammad learned the basic tenets of Islam. It was Djibril who revealed the Koran, the holy book of Islam, to Muhammad.

In Islam, angels can appear in different forms, especially in visions and dreams. Mary saw Djibril as a man (Koran 19:17). Angels visited Abraham in the form of men. However, most people are unable to determine what they look like.

Archangel Gabriel is credited with teaching Muhammad the essentials of the Muslim faith. In Islam, two angels, Munkar and Nakir, question individuals about their faith on the Day of Judgement. Djibril, the angel of revelation, relates to the Christian archangel Gabriel. Mikal, the Islamic angel of nature, can be related to Michael. Izrail is the Islamic angel of death, and Israfil is the angel who blows the trumpet on the Day of Judgement.

Muslims also believe in guardian angels. Surah 86, verse 4, of the Koran says, "There is no soul but has a protector over it." In fact, everyone has two guardian angels who watch over and record everything their charges do. One guardian angel watches over the person during the day, and the other one protects him or her during the night. In Islam, angels do not possess free will, and they perform only the tasks that God has ordered them to do. They do not, for instance, deliver prayers from humans to God.

Judaism, Christianity, and Islam are the three Abrahamic faiths, and all believe in the existence of angels. Angel-like beings appear in other religions, too.

Angels in Hinduism

In Hinduism there are no angels, but there are a number of spirit beings who act very much like angels. Hindus believe in *devas*, the "shining ones," who live on a higher plane to humans. They are benevolent spirits whose task is to motivate, protect, and encourage humankind. There are also *asuras*, who are evil spirits. They are fallen devas who live on a lower spiritual plane than the devas. Fortunately for them, they can be reincarnated into devas if they perform good deeds. They spend their time harming and impeding people's spiritual development.

Angels in Buddhism

Buddhists do not have angels, as such. However, they have devas, who are spiritual beings that usually appear as emanations of light. Devas are not involved in mankind's activities. However, they rejoice whenever a good deed is done anywhere in the world.

Good and Bad Angels

The Watchers (also known as Grigori) are an order of angels who had the task of teaching humanity. According to the first book of Enoch, about twelve thousand years ago, two hundred members of this order became attracted to human women and came down to earth on the peak of Mount Hermon, a mountain that was located about one hundred miles north of Jerusalem. They were nervous and worried about God's reaction to what they were proposing to do. Consequently, they made a pact that they would each have sexual relations with women. It took them a further nine days before they made contact with humans. Very quickly, each of the angels "defiled himself." In addition to this, they also taught women how to use makeup and decorate their bodies with gemstones, bracelets, and metal ornaments. They also taught people how to make and use weapons and provided techniques for divination. God was extremely unhappy with what these angels had done and ordered Gabriel to keep them imprisoned on earth until the Day of Judgment.

An intriguing passage in the book of Genesis alludes to these "sons of Gods" (Genesis 6:1–4). These were angels who fell in love with human women. The children of these marriages between angels and human women were called Nephilim. They were five-hundred-feet-tall giants who needed large amounts of food, and when this was scarce, they'd eat humans and even other Nephilim. Ultimately, God caused the Great Flood to eliminate them forever. Once they'd come down to earth, the Watchers were prohibited from ever returning to heaven.

In one version of the story, two angels, Shemhazai and Azael, were allowed to visit earth to see if mankind was commendable and good. However, the two angels were overcome with lust and slept with human women. Shemhazai admitted his sin and was turned into the constellation of Orion. Azael refused to repent and still offers trinkets and garments to women in the hope of leading men into sin. This is why Israel's sins are tossed over a cliff to him every year on the Day of Atonement.

Another story tells of a young virgin who resisted the approaches of these angels. She asked them to lend her wings. Once she had them, she flew to heaven and visited the Throne of God. After hearing her story, God transformed her into the constellation of Virgo.

How Many Angels Are There?

The logical answer to this question is "as many as necessary." However, people are not always logical, and a large number of possible numbers have been suggested. The Bible records that Daniel saw one hundred million angels in a vision (Daniel 7:10). When the prophet Enoch returned from heaven he said that he'd seen "angels innumerable, thousands of thousands, and myriads and myriads" (I Enoch 70:10). The Zohar says six hundred million angels were created on the second day of Creation (3:217a). However, additional angels were created on other occasions. Albert the Great, the Dominican monk who taught St. Thomas Aquinas, believed the total was almost four billion (Guiley 1996, 37). I still think the answer is "as many as necessary."

The War in Heaven

The war in heaven occurred when Lucifer, the most wise and beautiful angel of all, decided he no longer needed to accept the authority of God. In the book of Ezekiel, God speaks to Lucifer: "Thou wast perfect in thy ways from the day that thou wast created, till iniquity was found in thee" (Ezekiel 28:15).

The Prophet Isaiah described Lucifer's crime: "How art thou fallen from heaven, O Lucifer, son of the morning! how art thou cut down to the ground, which didst weaken the nations! For thou hast said in thine heart, I will ascend into heaven, I will exalt my throne above the stars of God" (Isaiah 14:12–13). It's possible that this passage by Isaiah was intended to describe the king of Babylon rather than Lucifer. However, as a result of it, the names Lucifer and Satan have become synonymous. In addition to these, the Devil has many other names, including Abaddon, Asmodeus, Beelzebub, Beliel, Dragon, Prince of Darkness, Serpent, and Snake.

Approximately one third of the angels in heaven joined Lucifer. In 1273, the Cardinal Bishop of Tusculum claimed this was 133,306,668 angels (Ronner 1993, 67). The person who counted them has never been identified.

Archangel Michael was placed in command of God's forces. A brief description of the battle can be found in the Revelation of St. John the Divine: "And there was war in heaven: Michael and his angels fought against the dragon; and the dragon fought and his angels, and prevailed not; neither was their place found any more in heaven. And the great dragon was cast out, that old serpent, called the Devil, and Satan, which deceiveth the whole world: he was cast out into the earth, and his angels were cast out with him" (Revelation 12:7–9).

Lucifer, now called Satan or the dragon, and his angels were cast into hell.

Despite suffering constant regret and pain as a result of what they had done, these angels are still scheming how to defeat heaven at the end of time. The fallen angels will be defeated again in this battle, and this time they'll all be destroyed.

In the Koran, there's an alternative account of why Lucifer was ordered out of heaven. Apparently, after God created humans, he ordered all the angels to bow down to, and serve, mankind. Lucifer (known as Iblis in the Koran) refused to do this. Lucifer believed that because angels were created from fire and humans from clay, he was better than humans. Because he refused to follow the word of God, Lucifer (Iblis) was ordered out of heaven (Koran 2:34; 7:11–18).

The story of Lucifer and the war in heaven is useful in Christianity as it provides an explanation for the existence of good and evil. God did not create good and bad angels. The fallen angels chose evil. Angels and humans both possess free will and have the ability to choose between good and evil. The fallen angels chose evil and are being punished for all eternity as a result.

two

The Hierarchy of Angels

A lthough angels were originally considered to be guides and guardians, during the early years of Christianity a number of writers (such as Saint Jerome, Saint Ambrose, Saint Gregory, and others) developed a hierarchy of angels that helped God achieve his purposes in the universe. Belief in a hierarchy of angels plays an important role in Christianity and Judaism but doesn't feature in other religions.

All organizations have a hierarchy, which means a system of people ranked one above another. They look like a pyramid with the CEO at the top and the most junior people at the bottom. In the hierarchy of angels the most important angels are those closest to God, and the least important ones are the ones closest to humans. A number of different classification systems were proposed by different people, such as Saint Ambrose, Saint Jerome, Saint Gregory, and John of Damascus. However, the system that came to be accepted by most angelologists was devised by Pseudo-Dionysius, who lived in the late fifth and early sixth centuries CE. In fact, it was Pseudo-Dionysius who coined the word "hierarchy." He used two Greek words, *hieros* ("sacred") and *arkhia* ("rule") to create his new word.

This unknown man with a Greek name was probably a Syrian monk. He claimed in his writings to be Saint Dionysius the Areopagite, who was converted to Christianity by Saint Paul. The real Dionysius later became the first bishop of Athens and a Christian martyr. However, the man who took his name lived many centuries after the real Dionysius. Although some people doubted the authenticity of his works from the beginning, it was not until the sixteenth century that people began questioning his authenticity, and he was generally considered to be the real Saint Dionysius until the twentieth century. Pseudo-Dionysius's motives are not known, but it's likely that he thought his ideas would achieve wider acceptance if he wrote as Saint Dionysius. This was a common practice in his lifetime, and there is no doubt that his writings achieved much greater prominence than they would have if he'd published them under his own name.

One of Pseudo-Dionysius's books was *The Celestial Harmony*, which quickly gained almost canonical status and retained it for almost a thousand years. Saint Thomas Aquinas, known as Doctor Angelus ("Angelic Doctor"), used Pseudo-Dionysius's ranking of angels in his book *Summa Theologica*, which is still a highly important book in Catholic theology. Dante Alighieri, the Italian poet and politician, made one change to Pseudo-Dionysius's list. In his epic poem *The Divine Comedy*, he changed the order of the archangels and principalities, making the archangels seventh and the principalities eighth in his list. Several eminent theologians, including Alan of Lille, Saint Bonaventure, John Duns Scotus, Hugh of Saint Victor, and Thomas Gallus wrote commentaries on Pseudo-Dionysius's work.

Pseudo-Dionysius defined a hierarchy as "a sacred order, a state of understanding and an activity approximating as closely as possible to the divine" (Pseudo-Dionysius 1987, 153). "The goal of a hierarchy," Pseudo-Dionysius wrote, "is to enable beings to be as like as possible to God and to be at one with him" (Pseudo-Dionysius, 1987, 154).

Pseudo-Dionysius was heavily influenced by Platonic and Neoplatonic thought, which revered the number three. Consequently, he started with the names of the traditional nine groups of angels. Although these nine orders are all mentioned by name in the Bible, no mention is made of their status or ranking. Pseudo-Dionysius arranged these nine orders into three groups of three, known as triads. Each of the three ranks of angels in each triad was then classified by three levels of intelligences. The first, or top, level is union or perfection, the second is illumination, and the third, purification. This system enables the divine spirit to descend into the world and also allows humans to reach up to heaven.

In this system, God is at the center, encircled by nine orders of angels. Every angel possesses the powers and capabilities of the angels in lower groups but not of those above them in the hierarchy. In *Paradiso*, the third part of *The Divine Comedy*, Dante wrote,

> And all these orders upward gaze with awe,
> And downward each prevails upon the rest,
> Whence all are drawn to God and to Him draw.
> (canto XXVIII, lines 128–130)

Triad One: The Angels Closest to God

Seraphim

The seraphim are the angels who are closest to God. The word "seraphim" comes from the Hebrew *sarap* which means "fire maker" or "the burning one." The seraphim are the angels of fire and light and can purify people with a flash of lightning. The only time seraphim are mentioned in the Bible is in Isaiah 6:2–7, where they are said to possess six wings and worship God unceasingly, twenty-four hours a day. They continuously call out, "Holy, holy, holy, is the Lord of hosts; the whole earth is full of his glory." These words still play a part in Jewish services today and are called the *Kadosh*. Some sources say the seraphim have four faces and wings that are a bright and luminous red. In the third book of Enoch the seraphim are said to have sixteen heads, four facing each cardinal direction. Saint Denis, bishop of Paris and a Christian martyr, called the seraphim "the princes of pure love." Not even members of the cherubim can look at the seraphim, as their divine, flaming light is so strong. Despite this, Saint Francis of Assisi saw a seraph and is the only person to have done so. The rulers of the seraphim are Archangels Michael, Seraphiel, and Metatron. Some of the other members of this order are Chamuel, Jehoel, Nathanael, and Samael.

Cherubim

The name cherubim comes from the Hebrew word *kerub*, which means "fullness of knowledge" or "outpouring of wisdom." According to Pseudo-Dionysius, the name cherubim signifies "the power to know and to see God" (Pseudo-Dionysius 1987, 205C). Cherubim with flaming swords guarded the east entrance to the Garden of Eden (Genesis 3:24). In the Christian tradition, God is said to be enthroned on cherubim who served as His chariot (Psalm 18:10; Ezekiel 10:1–22). Two carved, golden figures of two cherubim with outstretched wings provided symbolic protection over the Ark of the Covenant that contained the stone tablets on which the Ten Commandments were inscribed (Exodus 25:18–22).

The prophet Ezekiel had a vision in which he saw cherubim. He described them as having four faces: one each of a man, a lion, an ox, and an eagle. They also had four wings, feet like a calf, and hands like a man. They looked like "burning coals of fire," which fired bursts of lightning (Ezekiel 1, 41:18). Assyrian artists depicted the cherubim as winged beings with human or lion faces and the bodies of bulls, eagles, or sphinxes. Today they are usually depicted as tall men with two, four, or six blue wings. They are also frequently drawn as heads and wings but with no body.

The cherubim look after the sun, the moon, and the stars. They also look after the heavenly records and help people gain knowledge and divine wisdom. The cherubim enjoy detailed work and look after God's records. They also teach the lower orders of angels.

The leading members of the cherubim are Raphael, Gabriel, Ophaniel, Rikbiel, and Ophaniel. Other well-known members of the cherubim are Jophiel, Kerubiel, Uriel, and Zapiel. It's possible that Satan was a prince of the cherubim before his fall.

Thrones

In his vision, Ezekiel saw the thrones as huge fiery wheels full of eyes. These are the wheels of the chariot throne of God, known as the Merkavah. In fact, the thrones are often called wheels. Artists usually portray the thrones as large fiery wheels, with four wings that are completely covered with penetrating eyes. The thrones are always in God's presence and constantly chant glorias to him. According to the Testament of Adam, the thrones stand in front of the throne of God.

They are the angels of justice and administer divine justice to people on Earth to maintain the universal laws of the universe. They advise God before he makes important decisions. The thrones are peaceful, calm, and warm. Many people believe the Virgin Mary belongs to this order of angels. The leading members of the thrones are Jophiel, Orifiel, Raziel, and Zaphkiel.

Triad Two:
The Princes or Leaders of the Heavenly Kingdom
Dominions or Dominations

This group are often considered to be the oldest angels. Their job is to supervise the angels below them in the hierarchy. They issue the necessary commands to ensure the universe works the way it should. The seraphim, cherubim, and thrones do not need any supervision. The dominions carry a staff with a cross on top of it in their left hands and a seal bearing a monogram of Jesus in their right, to symbolize their power and authority. They are usually depicted wearing green and gold robes and with two wings. Despite their power, they are also angels of mercy. The leading members of this order are Hashmal, Muriel, Zacharael, and Zadkiel.

Virtues

Virtues carry out the wishes of the dominions and are in charge of all the natural laws of the universe. In Hebrew tradition, they're also responsible for the miracles that go against these laws. Saint Gregory the Great thought that God performed most of his miracles using the virtues. These angels help people who need courage and the ability to get along well with others. The virtues are often referred to as the "shining ones" or "radiant ones." According to the book of Adam and Eve, two virtues and twelve angels helped Eve when she was pregnant with Cain (Charles 1913, xxi:1). Two men "in white apparel" accompanied Jesus when he ascended into heaven (Acts 1:10). These men in white are generally believed to be members of the order of virtues. Members of the virtues also acted as midwives when Eve gave birth to Cain.

Christian artists usually depict virtues as bishops carrying a lily or a red rose that symbolizes the passion of Christ. They wear a golden belt around their waists.

Archangel Michael is prince regent of the choir of virtues. Leading members of this group include Barbiel, Cassiel, Gabriel, Peliel, Raphael, and Uzziel.

Powers

The name "powers" indicates that these angels possess powers that are well beyond those of humans. One of their tasks is to keep the akashic records and to protect people's souls. The powers prevent demons and other evil spirits from trying to overthrow the world. They are also highly courageous and, because of this, guard the pathways into heaven.

Artists usually portray members of the choir of powers as large men wearing armor and holding chained demons. They sometimes also hold a golden staff in their right hands.

Chamuel is usually considered chief of the choir of powers. However, some authorities claim that Gabriel, Raphael, or Verchiel rules this choir. Other leading members of this group include Camael and Sammael.

Triad Three: The Ministering Angels

Principalities

The principalities oversee and protect countries, cities, towns, and sacred sites. They also advise and guide religious leaders toward the truth. Another of their tasks is to motivate and help people's guardian angels in their work. Principalities were mentioned seven times by the Apostle Paul. They are good administrators who are involved in governing the universe (Romans 8:38; Ephesians 1:21, 3:10, 6:12; Colossians 1:16, 2:10, 2:15).

Members of the principalities are usually drawn wearing armor and a crown. The crown symbolizes the "prince" in the word principalities. They usually carry a cross, a scepter, or a sword.

According to John Milton, Nisroc is the chief angel of the principalities. Other leading members of this group include Amael, Anael, Cerviel, and Requel.

Archangels

Archangels are often called ruling angels. This is because they direct the will of God and control the seasons, the movement of the stars, the waters of the earth, and all plant and animal life. They also record all the incarnations of every person in the world. Another of their tasks is to supervise guardian angels. Archangels are God's most important messengers, and God uses them when he has extremely important messages to deliver to humans.

Two archangels are identified by name in the Bible. However, Michael is the only angel in the Bible who is clearly said to be an archangel. The first mention of Michael in the Bible is in Jude 9. In Daniel 10:13 he is described as "one of the chief princes." In Revelation 12:7–8 he is shown as God's warrior: "And there was war in heaven: Michael and his angels fought against the dragon; and the dragon fought and his angels, and prevailed not; neither was their place found any more in heaven." Because of this, the archangels are believed to command God's armies in the endless battle against evil.

The other archangel mentioned by name is Gabriel, who is clearly identified as God's messenger (Daniel 8:16, 9:21). Gabriel visited Zacharias and told him that his wife, Elizabeth, would bear him a son. He said, "I am Gabriel, that stand in the presence of God; and am sent to speak unto thee, and to shew thee these glad tidings" (Luke 1:19). Gabriel also appeared to Mary, the virgin who was espoused to Joseph, to tell her that she, too, would have a baby: "And in the sixth month the angel Gabriel was sent from God unto a city of Galilee, named Nazareth" (Luke 1:26).

Raphael protects and helps Tobias in the book of Tobit, which is part of the Catholic Bible.

The apostle John wrote that he saw the "seven angels who stood before God" (Revelations 8:2). Traditionally, these angels are thought to be the seven archangels. A number of people have suggested different angels for these roles. Raphael, Gabriel, Michael, and Uriel appear in most listings. Pseudo-Dionysius believed the archangels were Chamuel, Gabriel, Jophiel, Michael, Raphael, Uriel, and Zadkiel. This listing in the book of Enoch is the one that is usually accepted: Uriel, Raguel, Gabriel, Michael, Seraqael, Haniel, and Raphael. Judaism and Christianity recognize seven archangels; Islam recognizes four.

The only other mention of archangels in the Bible occurs in 1 Thessalonians 4:16, which says: "For the Lord himself will descend from heaven with a shout, with the voice of the archangel, and with the trump[et] of God." Raphael is said to be the prince of the archangels.

Angels

The angels in this group are the humble workers and are the angels closest to human beings. If the seraphim are generals, the angels are privates in God's army. The members of this group are the angels most likely to be seen by humans. There are millions of angels in this group, and although they have been frequently seen by people, they are not usually identified by name.

Angels have always been God's messengers. The word *angel* is derived from the Greek *angelos*, which means "messenger." In Hebrew, angels are called *mal'akh*, which means "messenger." They take people's prayers to God and also deliver the answers. They also deliver any messages that God might send to humans.

Why Are Archangels Ranked So Low?

Many people express surprise that archangels, who derive their name from the Greek word *archein*, which means "most important," "at the top," or "to rule," are listed second to bottom in the hierarchy of angels. In the hierarchy of angels the most important groups are listed closer to God. The least important ones were believed to be closer to mankind. Because, under special circumstances, people can see angels and archangels but not angels from higher ranks, archangels were listed immediately above angels.

The situation becomes more complicated, as Michael is considered to be captain of the host of the Lord, which makes him the most important angel of all. This problem arose because initially there were just two groups: angels and archangels. Over the centuries, scholars proposed different choirs of angels, until a number of hierarchies were created.

In the Greek *Testament of Levi*, written between 153 CE and 107 CE, both God and the archangels live in the highest Heaven (Charles 1908, 3:3–6).

three

Your Guardian Angels

Have you ever thought "Something told me not to do that" or "He seems nice, but I just don't trust him"? We all have a small, quiet voice inside our heads that guides and directs us. Many years ago, when I gave a series of talks at a maximum security prison, several prisoners told me that they'd heard a voice telling them not to do something but did it anyway. They now regretted not taking this advice. Is it possible that these messages are coming from our guardian angel?

Everyone has a guardian angel. They guide people from the day they're born to the very end of life. Some people believe that they start looking after their charges at the moment of conception. They provide protection, guidance, and companionship. Their ultimate goal is to help their charges' souls achieve salvation.

The concept of guardian angels is extremely old and began in ancient Mesopotamia, where people believed they had a personal god called *massar sulmi* ("guardian of people's safety"). The Zoroastrians called these protective beings *fravashis*. The ancient Greeks had their *daemons*, which were spirits that guided people through life. The Romans believed each man had a guardian spirit called a *genius* and every woman had a *juno*.

Guardian angels are mentioned in the Bible. When talking about children, Jesus said: "Take heed that ye despise not one of these little ones; for I say unto you, That in heaven their angels do always behold the face of my Father which is in heaven" (Matthew 18:10). David, the psalmist, wrote, "For he shall give his angels charge over thee, to keep thee in all thy ways. They shall bear thee up in their hands, lest thou dash thy foot against a stone" (Psalms 91:11–12).

In the Acts of the Apostles, Saint Paul saw his guardian angel when the ship he was a prisoner in was caught in a storm that lasted for days. His angel said, "And now I exhort you to be of good cheer: for there shall be no loss of any man's life among you, but of the ship" (Acts 27:22). This prophecy turned out to be correct. Everyone on board was saved, but the ship was destroyed. Saint Paul also wrote, "Are they not all ministering spirits, sent forth to minister for them who shall be heirs of salvation?" (Hebrews 1:14).

An interesting reference to a guardian angel is recorded in Acts 12:6–17. Saint Peter, who had been imprisoned by

King Herod, was woken one night by an angel. The chains that confined him fell off, and the angel escorted him outside to freedom. Initially, Peter thought he was experiencing a vision, and it was only when the angel vanished that he realised it had actually happened. Peter went to the house of Mary, the mother of John, where many people had gathered to pray. A young woman named Rhoda answered his knock at the gate and was excited to hear Peter's voice. She ran to tell the others, who said, "Thou art mad. … It is his angel" (Acts 12:15). Peter had to convince everyone that it really was him and not an angel.

The early Church fathers agreed about the reality of guardian angels. However, they couldn't decide whether or not heathens, or people that had not been baptized, had their own personal angels. They also couldn't agree about when guardian angels began looking after the people in their care. Saint Jerome wrote, "How great the dignity of the soul, since each one has from his birth an angel commissioned to guard it" (2008, xviii, lib II). Saint Anselm thought guardian angels were assigned before birth, as he wrote, "Every soul is committed to an angel when it is united with the body" (2008, part II, line 31).

Origen, a Christian theologian who wrote extensively about angels, believed that God passes the soul over to an angel as soon as the person converts to Christianity. He also believed that everyone had both a good and bad angel. The good angel guided the person, and the evil one offered temptation. This idea was a popular belief in Judaism, too.

In about 150 CE, a small book called *The Shepherd of Hermas* appeared. It became hugely popular and was even read in churches. It had a huge influence on believers for at least two hundred years. The shepherd of the title was actually Hermas' guardian angel. Hermas was a former slave who believed that we all have two angels: one who encourages us to do good, and another who tempts us toward evil (*The Shepherd of Hermas* [1926] 2009).

The concept of guardian angels was popular in the Middle Ages. Saint Thomas Aquinas was a firm believer in guardian angels and became known as the Angelic Doctor. He believed that guardian angels could leave their person temporarily but would never leave permanently, no matter what the person had done. He also believed that guardian angels stay with their charges even after death and stand next to them in heaven (part 1, question 113, article 4).

Padre Pio was a Catholic priest who experienced stigmata. This meant the signs of Christ's crucifixion appeared on his hands and feet. He first started seeing his guardian angel when he was a child. As an adult, his guardian angel was able to help him in many ways, including translating letters he'd received from people around the world who wanted his help. He was able to reply to these letters in the writers' own language. Father Parente wrote in his biography of Padre Pio, "Padre Pio's spiritual guidance of souls was mostly done through the help and direction of his Guardian Angel" (Parente 1984, 113). Padre Pio was declared a saint on June 16, 2002. Throughout his life, Padre Pio made a daily prayer to his guardian angel:

> *Angel of God,*
> *My guardian,*
> *To whom the goodness*

Of the Heavenly Father entrusts me.
Enlighten,
Protect and guide me
Now and forever,
Amen.

Pope Pius XI used his guardian angel to help resolve problems. Before any potentially difficult meetings he'd pray to his guardian angel, asking him to speak with the guardian angels of the people he was going to be dealing with to ensure that the meeting went well. Apparently, this worked extremely well. The two angels would resolve any problems, and the pope's meeting would be successful and free of discord.

A later pope, Pope John XXIII, frequently mentioned guardian angels in his radio talks. He constantly told parents to teach their children that they were never alone, as they had guardian angels looking after them (Guiley 1994, 59–60).

In 1968, Pope Paul VI sanctioned the establishment of the Opus Sanctorum Angelorum ("Work of the Holy Angels"). This organization, called Opus for short, has a number of aims that include fostering a belief in guardian angels. During their first year of study, the initiates promise God that they will love their guardian angels and act on their wishes. They also learn the names of their own personal guardian angels. In later stages, the initiates participate in a candlelit ceremony and promise to become like angels and to venerate angels. The final stage includes a ceremony of consecration dedicated to the entire angelic hierarchy.

In his Regina Caeli address on March 31, 1997, Pope John Paul II said, "Let us invoke the Queen of angels and saints, that she may grant us, supported by our guardian angels, to be authentic witnesses to the Lord's paschal mystery" (John Paul II).

Even though it's not part of the doctrine of the Catholic Church, Catholics believe that everyone has a guardian angel who has the task of watching over and protecting their charge. On October 2, the Roman Catholic Church celebrates the Feast of the Guardian Angels. A popular Catholic prayer that is taught to children goes,

> *Angel of God, my guardian dear,*
> *To whom God's love commits me here,*
> *Ever this day [or night], be at my side,*
> *To light and guard, to rule and guide.*
> *Amen.*

This prayer is not just for children. Pope John XXIII said this prayer five times every day.

What Do Guardian Angels Do?

In the Christian tradition the main task of a guardian angel is to ensure that the soul leads a good life and ultimately gets to heaven. Most people know that guardian angels guide and protect the souls they have been assigned to. However, they also have other tasks.

1. They do their best to help the soul achieve salvation. This can be achieved through the grace of a deity or through the prayers and good deeds of the person.

2. They provide protection when the soul is in danger. For most people, this would be protection from difficulties in the physical world, but guardian angels also

provide protection from the "snare of the devil" (2 Timothy 2:26).

3. They encourage good thoughts and deeds. Usually, the soul is not aware that his or her guardian angel is gently encouraging the person to think good thoughts and to do the right thing. If this influence is noticed at all, it will usually come in the form of an intuition or thought. It can sometimes be felt as the voice of conscience. On October 2, 2014, Pope Francis said that when we have a feeling that "'I should do this, this is not right, be careful,'" it "is the voice of" our guardian angel or "travelling companion" (Schneible 2014). However, your guardian angel can help you only if you're willing to listen and take advice. Your guardian angel will not override your free will.

4. Guardian angels pray with their charges. Many people believe that guardian angels interweave their prayers with that of their souls to make the prayers more effective and more pleasing to God.

5. Guardian angels correct people's souls when they have strayed. If someone has veered from the path of honesty and good deeds, his or her guardian angel will do everything possible to encourage the person to reevaluate his or her life and to return to the path of righteousness.

6. Guardian angels reveal the will of God. A good example of this is recorded in Genesis 22:9–18, in which an angel prevented Abraham from sacrificing Isaac and told him of the huge influence his descendants would have on the world. He explained, "And in thy seed

shall all the nations of the earth be blessed; because thou hast obeyed my voice" (Genesis 2:18).

7. Guardian angels continuously praise God and encourage their charges to do the same.

8. Guardian angels strengthen and comfort people when they are suffering.

9. Guardian angels protect and help souls at the moment of death. In the Catholic tradition, guardian angels regularly visit their charges if they go to purgatory. Once these souls have been purified of all their sins, their guardian angels will escort them to heaven. Mary, Queen of the Angels, decides when the souls are ready.

Unfortunately, few people are aware of everything their guardian angel is doing for them. Saint Ignatius of Loyola, the founder of the Jesuits (Society of Jesus), said that people had to advance spiritually before they could feel and experience the faint, gentle, yet insistent energy of their angels.

How to Experience Your Guardian Angel

Many people expect to see their guardian angels. In their imaginations, they see their guardian angels dressed in white robes, surrounded by a pure white light, and possibly holding a harp. In actuality, few people are able to see their guardian angels, but everyone can learn to experience their guardian angel. This can happen in a variety of ways.

Knowing

This often occurs when the person experiences a sense of well-being and protection. They suddenly know that their guardian angel is always with them and will keep them safe.

A friend of mine experienced her guardian angel while living alone in London. She couldn't find work and lived in constant fear of being evicted from her tiny room in a boarding house. She was too proud to ask relatives for help, and because she had no money, her social life dwindled away to nothing. One day, while walking to yet another job interview, she suddenly knew that she was accompanied by a presence, which she later realized was her guardian angel. This gave her immediate confidence, and for the first time in her life she didn't feel nervous during the job interview. Two days later, she was called back for a second interview and immediately afterward was offered the position. Today, many years later, she still communicates with her guardian angel every day and credits all the good things that have happened to her to her special angel.

Dreams

Many people experience their guardian angel in their dreams. As our dreams help us understand what's going on in our lives, it's not surprising that our guardian angel can appear in them. This usually happens randomly, but it's possible to encourage your guardian angel to speak to you in your dreams by repeating to yourself as you drift off to sleep, "Soon my guardian angel will appear in my dreams."

It's a good idea to keep a dream diary by your bed. This enables you to write down everything you remember about your dream as soon as you wake up, before it fades away as you start on your day. I like to lie in bed for a few minutes, without changing position, and see how much I can recall. Once I've done this, I get up and write it down. This is a good way to record your experiences with your guardian angel. However, you'll find your dreams will also prove helpful in other ways, as they provide insights and information about all areas of your life.

Thoughts and Feelings

Our guardian angels frequently communicate with us through our thoughts and feelings. Obviously, most of our thoughts and feelings do not come from our guardian angel. However, every now and again, we experience a thought or feeling that we know has come from a source other than our own minds. Many creative people experience this on a regular basis, and I believe their "inspiration" has come from their guardian angel.

People who achieve great success in the business world also experience this type of feeling, and it is what has helped guide them to success in their chosen fields. A friend of mine is extremely good at building up businesses and selling them at the perfect time to achieve the maximum amount of money for them. He has done this at least a dozen times over the last twenty years and happily tells everyone that a small voice tells him which businesses to buy and when it's time to sell.

Intuition

Intuition is closely related to thoughts and feelings. We all receive intuitive hunches from time to time. A good way to allow intuition to flow is to set aside quiet times where you can pause and wait to see what your intuitive mind is willing to share with you. Any repetitive action that doesn't involve conscious thought can also encourage your intuition. Whenever I have a problem with my writing, I go for a walk. I don't think a great deal about the writing while I'm enjoying the walk, but, almost always, when I sit down to my computer again, the answer will be in my mind. I believe this is my guardian angel helping me.

I was recently told an interesting story by an acquaintance who is the public relations manager of a large company. He had interviewed several people for an important role in the company. Logic told him to employ a particular candidate who had impressed him greatly in the interviews. On the way home from work, he decided to contact this applicant in the morning to tell him he had the position. However, during the evening, when he wasn't thinking about work, he suddenly received an intuition that one of the other applicants would be better. This was someone he'd dismissed from his mind early on in the interviewing process, and he was confused and puzzled by his intuition. His wife told him to follow his intuition, and he rather reluctantly took her advice. This applicant did an excellent job for the company, and three months later, the person he'd nearly employed was arrested for stealing money from his previous employer. My acquaintance credited his good decision to an intuition from his guardian angel. "It had to be my guardian angel, as he was protecting and helping me," he told me.

Prayer

Prayer is another good way to make contact with your guardian angel. All you need do is to pray in your normal manner. In the course of your prayers, ask for help to contact your guardian angel. Once you've made contact, you can speak to your guardian angel whenever you wish, simply by making a prayer. As mentioned earlier, Pope Pius XI prayed to his guardian angel every morning and evening. He'd also pray to his guardian angel during the day if he felt it necessary.

Coincidences, Synchronicity, and Serendipity

On more than one occasion I've accidentally dropped a book on the floor and, when I bent to pick it up, found that it was lying open to pages that covered exactly what I was looking for. Consequently, whenever I experience a coincidence, synchronicity, or serendipity, I pause for a moment or two to see if my guardian angel is behind it. Sometimes a coincidence will be simply that, but at other times it happens at exactly the right moment, and I'll know there is more to it than simply a coincidence.

Draw Your Guardian Angel

Fortunately, no artistic skill is necessary for this method, as you'll be the only person who sees what you produce. All forms of creativity can be enhanced when you ask your guardian angel for help. You can also use your creativity to help you experience your guardian angel.

Sit down somewhere and start drawing angels. Use a variety of colors, and do the best work you can. When you focus on drawing angels, you'll attract your guardian angel to you. Your guardian angel is likely to start influencing the movements of your pen, and you may find the quality of your work gets better and better.

Remain Aware

Your guardian angel is constantly with you and wants to help. Because of this, a good way to experience your guardian angel is to simply accept that he or she is with you and speak to your guardian angel. Speak in your normal manner, as if you were talking to a close friend. Ask your angel for anything you need. Make sure that your requests are framed clearly. Once you've made your request, remain calm and confident that your guardian angel will be doing whatever is necessary for you to receive whatever it is you have asked for. Realize that it will not usually simply land in your lap. You'll probably have to work hard for it, but your guardian angel will provide the necessary opportunities so that you can achieve your goal.

Does Your Guardian Angel Have a Name?

Your guardian angel has a name and is willing to tell you what it is, if you ask for it. You can do this in a variety of ways. You might find a quiet spot in a park or in the countryside where you can relax and commune with nature. Sit or lie down, and think peaceful thoughts for twenty or thirty minutes. Once you feel totally relaxed, think about your guardian angel for a minute or two. Think about everything he or she does for you, most of which you aren't aware of and don't notice. After silently expressing your gratitude, say hello to your guardian angel. Wait silently. I find it helpful to pay attention to my breathing while waiting for a response. You may hear an almost imperceptible hello as your guardian angel replies. You mightn't hear anything but instead receive an intuition that your guardian angel has responded. Once you've made contact, you can ask your guardian angel anything you wish to know. The responses are likely to come into your mind as thoughts or feelings, making it hard to tell if they're replies from your angel or your own mind talking. If you're enjoying a conversation with your guardian angel, these thoughts are likely to be your angel's replies. Most of the time you'll "know" when your guardian angel is talking to you. If you're naturally intuitive, you'll have a feeling or sense of knowing when your guardian angel is talking to you.

When you feel ready, ask your angel to tell you his or her name. You may not receive a response to this immediately. The reply might come to you in the form of a dream, or you may suddenly see or read a particular name everywhere you go. Initially, you may put this down to coincidence, but if the same name keeps on reccurring, you'll know it was a message from your guardian angel. This can also happen, even when your guardian angel told you his or her name. It's similar to buying a car and suddenly seeing that particular brand and model everywhere you go.

Here are some other ways you can use to converse with your guardian angel:

1. You can communicate with your guardian angel in your dreams. Before going to sleep, think about the different questions you want to ask your guardian angel. I find it helpful to write these down, so I can read through the list before going to sleep. Several people I know place these questions under their pillow, as they believe they'll receive a quicker response if they "sleep on it."

When you wake up in the morning, lie as still as you can for a minute or two, and see what memories your guardian angel has placed in your mind. It's a good idea to record these as soon as you get up. I use a dream diary, which I keep beside my bed, but you can record the answers on a cell phone or digital recorder.

2. You can create a magic circle in your living room or anywhere else you won't be disturbed for at least twenty minutes. You can imagine the circle and place candles at the north, south, east, and west positions. Light the candles, and sit down comfortably in the middle of the circle. I used to be able to make myself comfortable sitting on the floor, but nowadays I sit on a chair. Close your eyes, and visualize the circle completely surrounding you, as if you were sitting inside a huge, magical tube. Visualize this tube gradually filling up with a pure, white light, until you're totally surrounded by it. Think about your guardian angel, and ask him or her if this is a good time for you to ask some questions. Wait for a response, and then, if the time is right, enjoy your conversation.

3. Lie flat on your back on the floor, close your eyes, and take several slow deep breaths. With each exhalation, say silently, "Relax, relax, relax." When you feel ready, start relaxing your body by focusing your attention on your left foot and willing it to relax. Repeat with your right foot, and gradually move up through your body to the top of your head. Once you feel totally relaxed, think about the most beautiful and restful place you have ever seen. You might think of a place you know,

or you might create a magnificent and restful picture in your mind. Picture yourself inside this beautiful scene, and know that your guardian angel is with you. Start by saying hello, and then enjoy a pleasant conversation with your guardian angel.

4. Sit down in a straight-backed chair, close your eyes, and make interlocking circles with your thumbs and forefingers. This creates a circle of protection. Rub the tips of your thumbs and forefingers together, and send a silent message to your guardian angel. This is a quicker method than the others and is a good one to use if you need to communicate with your guardian angel quickly or if you're doing the exercise somewhere where you won't have much time on your own. I've used this method several times on buses and trains, and none of the other passengers noticed or had any idea what I was doing.

5. Another good way to converse with your guardian angel is to do something you particularly enjoy. This could be gardening, cooking, exercising, playing a musical instrument, or reading a book. At some stage while you're enjoying whatever it is that you're doing, pause and say hello to your guardian angel. Enjoy the conversation, and once it's over, return to your hobby or interest. This method works well, as you're in the perfect frame of mind for angelic communication when you're lost in something you particularly enjoy.

Many angel names come from Hebrew and are difficult for Westerners to pronounce. Consequently, when your guardian angel tells you his or her name, you might be surprised as it is such an ordinary name. This is done deliberately, when your guardian angel thinks you might have difficulty in comprehending his actual name.

How to Communicate with Your Guardian Angel

You can communicate with your guardian angel whenever you wish. By far the best way is to enjoy frequent conversations with your angel. This is much more effective than calling on your angel only when you're in trouble and need help. The following are several ways to enhance your communications with your guardian angel. You may find one method works well for you and you won't need to experiment with the others, or you might choose whichever method feels right for you at the moment.

Prayer

Every morning and night say a prayer to your guardian angel. You might start with the "Angel of God, my guardian dear" prayer and then carry on with a prayer of your own. This prayer needn't be formal. Simply talk to your guardian angel as if he or she were a close friend, which, in fact, is the case. Pause at regular intervals to receive a response, and then continue with the conversation. When it's time to finish the conversation, thank your guardian angel for everything he or she does for you, and say goodbye.

Write a Letter

Sit down somewhere quiet and peaceful, and write a friendly, chatty letter to your guardian angel. Write about your problems and concerns, of course, but also include information about what's going on in your life. Write about your family and friends. Write about your hopes and dreams and some of the pleasant activities you've recently enjoyed. Express gratitude for all the blessings in your life. When you've finished your letter, express your love for your guardian angel and sign your name. Place it in an envelope, address it to your guardian angel, seal it—and then burn it. Gather up the ashes and scatter them outdoors. You should make a ritual or ceremony around the burning of your letter. Visualize the smoke sending your letter directly to your guardian angel. Quite apart from anything else, writing a letter is a good way to sort out your problems and to see matters in perspective.

Create an Altar

Find a place where you can communicate with your guardian angel regularly, without being concerned about being disturbed. Your altar can be any flat surface. Place on it anything that reminds you of spiritual matters. You might like to add one or two candles, crystals, and small ornaments. Look after your spiritual space, and use it whenever you communicate with your angel.

Keep an Angel Journal

Keeping an angel journal enables you to keep track of all your communications with your guardian angel over a period of time. This will become increasingly valuable to you over a period of time. You can write anything you wish in your journal. Before starting my journal entries, I like to record the date, time of day, and where I happen to be. Writing in a journal is similar to writing your guardian angel a letter, except it usually doesn't include the news about family and loved ones. Record as much of your conversations as possible, and go back over them regularly to see how you're progressing. You'll find that your journal will feel increasingly spiritual the more you use it.

Contemplation

A contemplative prayer is one in which you wait quietly and listen for a message from the divine. It is a mixture of prayer and meditation. People who practice contemplative prayer report that they have a more intense experience of God than people who use other forms of prayer (Poloma 1991, 62). As a contemplative prayer takes at least thirty minutes to perform, few people have the time to practice it on a regular basis. You can also use contemplation to communicate with your guardian angel.

Sit down quietly, close your eyes, and take three slow, deep breaths. Visualize a peaceful scene, and allow yourself to relax. You might find it helpful to silently say a brief prayer to your guardian angel at this point. Once you've done this, continue waiting silently and expectantly. Dismiss any random, extraneous thoughts that come into your mind, but remain aware that your guardian angel is likely to communicate with you through your thoughts. Consequently, you need to evaluate your thoughts before dismissing them. Fortunately, if you do happen to dismiss a thought sent from your guardian angel, he or she will send it to you again, usually with more force than the first time. Once you've made contact with your guardian angel, listen carefully. Communicating with him or her through contemplation takes time and effort, but the insights and help you'll gain make everything worthwhile. You'll know when the session is over when your guardian angel stops talking, and you'll find yourself again in a state of peaceful silence. Say thank you and pray before taking three slow, deep breaths and opening your eyes.

How to Create Your Guardian Angel

Carl Jung wrote that angels were "nothing but the thoughts and intuitions of their Lord" (Jung 1963, 302). Evidently, Jung believed God was creating angels by using thought and intuition. Thomas Aquinas seemed to believe that angels were thought forms when he wrote, "Angels are composed of the ambient air of the place where they appear, which they arrange and condense into an appropriate form" (quoted in Evans 1987, 45). The eminent angelologist Gustav Davidson wrote, "I am prepared to say if enough of us believe in angels, the angels exist" (Davidson 1967, xii).

Our thoughts and feelings create thought forms all the time. A good example of a deliberately created thought form is a prayer. Naturally, there is no point in praying if the person doesn't believe that the prayer is being heard. When people pray, they create what Theosophists call a thought form.

Thought forms are concentrated parcels of energy. We all have fifty or sixty thousand thoughts a day. These can be pictured as thousands of small parcels attached to a long piece of rope. Most of the time, we have no control over our thoughts. One thought leads us to another, which then prompts something else, and so on.

Recently, while my wife and I were on vacation, we woke up to the smell of freshly baked bread. This immediately made me think of other occasions in the past when I also smelled freshly baked bread. I then thought of the delicious full grain bread that a neighbor used to make, and suddenly I was five years old again and walking home from the shops with a large loaf of bread. I remember that incident well, as my mother wasn't impressed to receive a half loaf—I'd eaten the rest while walking home. This is an example of the random way our thoughts work.

It would be extremely unlikely that anyone else would be able to pick up those thoughts, as they're fleeting impressions that have little energy or emotion attached to them. However, a vitally important thought, such as a major concern or a prayer, would create a powerful thought form.

When Charles Dickens, the famous author, was writing his books, he created his characters so powerfully that they became thought forms that affected every aspect of his life. James T. Fields said of Dickens, "He told me that when he was writing *The Old Curiosity Shop* the creatures of his imagination haunted him so much that they would neither let him sleep or eat in peace" (Fodor 1933, 382).

Factors of a Thought Form

You need to be able to construct a powerful thought form to create your guardian angel. These four factors are involved: emotion, focus, relaxation, and attraction.

Emotion

When emotion is added to a thought, it becomes vibrant and unforgettable. You can prove this for yourself by thinking about a negative experience you had when you were very young. As you think about it, all the emotions that occurred at the time will come back to you, even though the experience may have happened many decades ago. Now think about something exciting that occurred to you as an adult. Again, all the emotions will come back to you, as the experience was so memorable and important. Finally, think about a minor incident that happened a day or two ago. As it was unimportant and there was no emotion attached to it, it might be hard to think of anything.

It's fortunate that our memories work this way. If we remembered absolutely everything that happened to us all the time, our brains would quickly become overwhelmed and unable to function. This is why unimportant things are hardly noticed and may not even reach our conscious awareness.

To create an effective thought form we need to put as much emotion as possible into it. In fact, the more emotion that can be added, the greater the effect will be.

Focus

You also need to be able to focus clearly on your goal, which in this case is to create your guardian angel. If you can visualize your angel in your mind, you'll be able to focus and concentrate on this goal.

Relaxation

You need to be as relaxed as possible to consciously create a thought form. If you have any problems or concerns on your mind, you need to resolve them before starting. You also need a quiet, relaxing environment. Set aside time when you know there'll be few distractions. Make sure the room is warm enough, temporarily disconnect your phone, wear loose-fitting clothes, and be prepared to relax as much as you can.

Attraction

The Law of Attraction says that you attract to you whatever it is you think about. If you focus on poverty and lack, that is what you'll attract into your life. Similarly, if you focus on happiness and abundance, you'll attract them to you. You can do this consciously, by deliberately changing any negative thoughts as soon as you become aware of them. I know a number of people who have literally changed their lives by doing this. Because of the Law of Attraction, you need to create good affirmative thought forms by sending out good-quality, positive thoughts and emotions.

The Creation Process

It's now time to start work on creating your guardian angel.

1. Prepare the space you'll be working within. Make sure the room is the right temperature, close the blinds or curtains, and switch off your phone. You might like to play some meditation music. If you do this, don't play any recognizable songs or anything by a favorite singer, as these are likely to be distracting. You can buy New Age, relaxation, or stress-reducing CDs online or at New Age stores. You might like to burn incense and light candles. If you do this, you'll need to place them carefully to avoid any risk of fire. I like to use four white candles placed to indicate the four cardinal directions. When I do this, I work in the middle of an imaginary circle with the candles on the circumference. Choose a comfortable chair. A recliner chair is ideal. Lying

down in bed to do this exercise is not a good idea, as you're likely to fall asleep. I fall asleep very easily, and learned long ago to only ever do exercises of this sort in a comfortable chair. The final part of the preparation is to wear comfortable, loose-fitting clothes.

2. Sit or lie down in your chair and close your eyes. When you remove one of your senses, you heighten the others. It also eliminates the possibility of being distracted by suddenly noticing something in the room. It's also easier to visualize something when your eyes are closed.

3. Allow yourself to become as relaxed as possible. There are many ways to do this. The most common method is called progressive relaxation. Start by taking five slow deep breaths, holding each inhalation for a few moments before exhaling slowly. Forget about your breathing and focus on the toes of your left foot. Visualize them relaxing as much as possible. You might find they tingle slightly as you focus on them. Once they are fully relaxed, allow the relaxation to drift into your foot. Repeat this with your other foot. Once both feet are completely relaxed, allow the pleasant relaxation to drift into your ankles and up one leg, followed by the other. There's no need to hurry with any of this. Take as long as necessary with each part of your body. Once your legs are completely relaxed, allow the relaxation to drift up through your abdomen, chest, and shoulders. Allow one arm to relax completely, and then relax the other arm. Follow this by relaxing your neck and face. Allow

your eyes to relax, and allow the relaxation to drift up to the top of your head. Mentally scan your entire body, and spend as long as necessary relaxing any areas that are not yet completely relaxed.

Another relaxation technique is to tense all the muscles in one arm, and then let go and allow the arm to relax. Continue doing this with your other arm and each leg in turn. Once your arms and legs are relaxed, allow your body, neck, and head to relax.

One of my favorite methods is to raise both arms. Mentally count from five down to one. At the count of one allow your arms to drop to your sides or into your lap, and allow your entire body to relax. You can relax your entire body in a matter of seconds using this technique.

Yet another method is to focus on relaxing the muscles around your eyes. These are the finest muscles in your entire body. Once these muscles feel totally relaxed, you'll probably find that all the muscles in your body have relaxed too. If not, allow the pleasant relaxation around your eyes to spread throughout your entire body.

These are all methods that I use. If you haven't practiced relaxation techniques before, the best method to start with is the progressive relaxation. It takes longer than the other methods, but ensures that you become totally relaxed. Once you've become familiar with this method, experiment with the others.

Once you feel totally relaxed, you're ready to move on to the next stage.

4. Become aware of the stillness, peace, and tranquillity all around you. Mentally scan your body to ensure that you are completely relaxed, and give any extra attention to any areas that are not totally relaxed.

5. Once you're completely relaxed, visualize the back of your right hand. If you happen to be left-handed, picture your left hand. "See" the back of your hand in as much detail as possible. Once you can visualize the back of your hand, mentally turn it over so you can see the palm. See it as vividly as you can. Picture the main lines and the tiny skin ridge patterns. As you're mentally picturing your hand, see it for the wonder and miracle that it is.

   Take as long as you need to do this. When you feel ready, turn the hand over in your mind and focus on your thumb. Allow your focus to narrow until you're gazing at your thumbnail. Allow your thumbnail to grow until it is all you can see. Your thumbnail is the screen that we'll use to project your thought form on.

6. Visualize your guardian angel. See him or her as clearly as you can in your mind. You may find your mind wandering at this stage. If, and when, this happens, visualize your thumbnail again. When you can see it clearly, picture your guardian angel again. This may occur several times. It's perfectly natural for our minds to wander, and there's no need to be concerned when it happens.

   Your visualization of your guardian angel is unique to you. You might see a cute little cherub.

It could be a tall, slim angel wearing beautiful robes. Your angel may or may not have wings. Your angel might be a bright, shimmering light that expresses divine love. You may not "see" anything but simply have an impression or awareness that your guardian angel is there. Use your imagination and allow your inner mind to create whatever angel is right for you.

The image you create will be determined by your background and upbringing. Someone from a religious family is likely to imagine a traditional-looking guardian angel with large, pure white wings and flowing robes that are dazzling white. Someone with a nonreligious background may picture something completely different. It makes no difference what angel comes into your mind. The image you create is the perfect one for you. Visualize it as clearly as you possibly can.

7. You may not get this far on your first experiments at creating your guardian angel. It doesn't matter how many attempts you make, as each time you'll get a little bit closer to the desired result.

Once you can clearly see your guardian angel in your mind, you need to turn this picture into a thought form. Allow the image of your guardian angel to disappear and be replaced with a picture of your thumbnail. Once you can see your thumbnail in your mind, allow it to disappear and be replaced by your guardian angel. Switch from one to the other several times. Each time you do this you'll notice that you'll gradually get faster and faster at switching from one to the other.

8. It's now time to fill your guardian angel with emotion. Think of a time in your life when you felt safe, secure, completely happy, and surrounded by love. If you've never experienced feelings of this sort, imagine how wonderful it must be. Allow these feelings to completely surround you and fill you with pure, ineffable love.

   Enjoy these feelings for a minute or two. When you feel ready, visualize your guardian angel again. Because of the switching process you did in step 7, this should be easy to do. This time you need to switch from your guardian angel to the feelings of perfect love several times. This imprints the powerful emotion of perfect love into your guardian angel.

9. When you reach this stage, relax and observe your guardian angel. The image is likely to become clearer, and you'll be able to sense your angel reflecting love back to you. It's likely that your guardian angel will start to reveal his or her personality and may surprise you with what he or she does. Enjoy watching this, and interact with your angel as much as you can.

10. You've now reached the stage where you set your guardian angel free. This angel has been at least partially constructed by your imagination, and you have added love and consciousness to it. Your guardian angel has also developed individuality. Consequently, although he or she will always act in your

best interests, your angel may not always choose to do what you want it to.

11. Become aware of your thumbnail again. Gradually allow your view to expand until you can see your hand clearly. Mentally turn it over so your palm faces upward. Visualize your guardian angel standing on the palm of your hand.

    Gaze at your angel for a few moments and then thank it for being there for you. Send as much love as you can to him or her, and visualize the love being absorbed. Finally, in your mind, bring your open palm up to your lips and blow gently. Watch your angel rise off your hand and fly upward.

12. Spend a few moments thinking about what you've accomplished before returning to your everyday world. Slowly count from one to five, open your eyes, and stretch. When you feel ready, get up and continue with your day.

It's unusual for anyone to complete this exercise on the first attempt. Most people need to repeat it several times before they achieve the desired results. There's no need to be concerned if it takes longer than you expect. Remain patient, and you'll achieve success when you least expect it.

Is It Real?

I've been asked this question hundreds of times over the years. I find the best answer is to respond with another question: "Does your guardian angel seem real?"

The person always says, "Yes."

"Does your constructed guardian angel look after you?"

"Yes."

"Does it give you love, comfort, and protection?"

"Yes."

"In that case, does it matter if your constructed guardian angel is real or not?"

"No."

I believe that constructed guardian angels are real. When you create a thought form, you create a living parcel of energy that is loving, healing, and nurturing. Carl Jung described this process when he wrote that "angels personify the coming into consciousness of something new arising from the deep unconscious." Meister Eckhart, the German theologian, thought that angels represented the "ideas of God" (Nichols 1980, 251).

Once you've demonstrated for yourself the reality of your thought form–created guardian angel, you might like to create thought forms for other purposes. You may, for instance, send out thought forms of forgiveness, healing, and love to your friends and anyone who you think will benefit from them. The recipients may not know who sent them the thought forms, but they'll experience the feelings and will appreciate the benefits. You, in turn, will experience the pleasure and satisfaction of doing something worthwhile and valuable for the people you love.

The Schemhamphora Guardian Angels

The Schemhamphoras (or Schemhamphorae) are a group of seventy-two angels who bear the different names that have been given to God in the Jewish scriptures. They were first mentioned in the book of Exodus in the Bible: "Behold, I send an Angel before thee, to keep thee in the way, and to bring thee into the place which I have prepared. Beware of him, and obey his voice, provoke him not; for he will not pardon your transgressions: for my name is in him" (Exodus 23:20–21). The seventy-two names of angels come from Exodus 14:19–21. Each of these three verses contain seventy-two Hebrew letters that are arranged in various ways to create the names of seventy-two angels. These seventy-two names compose the name of God.

These names were believed to possess special spiritual power, and magicians today still invoke them in their rituals. In Kabbalistic teachings, these seventy-two Schemhamphoras angels are taught to be guiding or guardian angels. Here are the dates and the angels that relate to them:

Aries
March 21–25: Vehuiah
March 26–30: Jelial
March 31–April 4: Sitael
April 5–9: Elemiah
April 10–14: Mahasiah
April 15–20: Lelahel

Taurus
April 21–25: Achaiah
April 26–30: Cahatel
May 1–5: Haziel
May 6–10: Aladiah
May 11–15 (also June 11–15): Lauviah
May 16–20 (also July 17–22): Hahaiah

Gemini

May 21–25: Iezalel
May 26–31: Mebahel
June 1–5: Hariel
June 6–10: Hakamiah
June 11–15 (also May 11–15): Lauviah
June 16–21: Caliel

Cancer

June 22–26: Leuviah
June 27–July 1: Pahaliah
July 2–6: Nelchael
July 7–11: Ieiaeil (Jelalel)
July 12–16: Melahel
July 17–22 (also May 16–20): Hahajah

Leo

July 23–27: Nith-Haiah
July 28–August 1: Haaiah
August 2–6: Terathel
August 7–12: Seheiah
August 13–17: Reiiel
August 18–22: Omael

Virgo

August 23–28: Lecabel
August 29–September 2: Vasiariah
September 3–7: Yehudiah
September 8–12: Lehahiah
September 13–17: Chavakiah
September 18–23: Menadel

Libra

September 24–28: Anael

September 29–October 3: Haamiah

October 4–8: Rehael

October 9–13: Ieiazel

October 14–18: Hahahel

October 19–23: Mikael

Scorpio

October 24–28: Veualiah

October 29–November 2: Ielahiah

November 3–7: Sealiah

November 8–12: Ariel

November 13–17: Asaliah

November 18–22: Mihael

Sagittarius

November 23–27: Vahuel

November 28–December 2: Daniel

December 3–7: Hahasiah

December 8–12: Imamiah

December 13–16: Nanael

December 17–21: Nithael

Capricorn

December 22–26: Mebahiah

December 27–31: Poiel

January 1–5: Nemamiah

January 6–10: Ieilael

January 11–15: Harahel

January 16–20: Mitzrael

Aquarius

January 21–25: Umabel
January 26–30: Iahhel
January 31–February 4: Anauel
February 5–9: Mehiel
February 10–14: Damabiah
February 15–19: Manakel

Pisces

February 20–24: Eiael
February 25–29: Habuhiah
March 1–5: Rochel
March 6–10: Gabamiah
March 11–15: Haiaiel
March 16–20: Mumiah

You can call on your Schemhamphoras guardian angel whenever you need comfort, help, advice, or love. As your angel's name contains letters that form part of the name of God, this guardian angel has a special connection to the divine that will sometimes provide you with instant results.

four

The Archangels

The prefix *arch-* comes from the Greek word for "chief." Only three angels were mentioned by name in the Bible, and two of these are the archangels Michael and Gabriel. The other named angel is Lucifer. However, Michael is the only angel who is described as an archangel in the Bible (Jude 9). The seven angels who stood before God in the book of Revelation are usually thought to be the seven archangels (Revelation 15–17). These angels are Michael, Gabriel, Raphael, Uriel, Raguel, Sariel, and Remiel. Michael, Gabriel, Raphael, and Uriel are considered the most important of these and are described as the "Four Angels of the Presence." The first and third books of Enoch also refer to seven archangels. Raphael described himself as "one of the seven holy angels who present the prayers of the saints and enter into the presence of the glory of the Holy One" (Tobit 12:15).

The seven archangels were named for the first time when the prophet Enoch described his visit to the heavens in the second century BCE in the first book of Enoch; they are Uriel, Raphael, Raguel, Michael, Zerachiel, Gabriel, and Remiel.

Over the centuries, different people created lists of the angels they considered to be archangels. The list in the Testament of Solomon is Mikael, Gabriel, Uriel, Sabrael, Arael, Iaoth, and Adonael.

Saint Gregory the Great thought the seven archangels are Michael, Gabriel, Raphael, Uriel, Simiel, Orifiel, and Zachariel.

Dionysius the Areopagite listed Michael, Gabriel, Raphael, Uriel, Chamuel, Jophiel, and Zadkiel.

In addition to the angels mentioned in these lists, many other angels have been called archangels. These include Adnachiel, Anael, Asmodel, Barchiel, Cambiel, Cassiel, Hamaliel, Khamael, Malkhidael, Metatron, Mizrael, Perpetiel, Raziel, Sachiel, Sahaqiel, Salaphiel, Samael, Sandalphon, Saraqael, Sariel, Sidrael, Suriel, Tzaphiel, Verchiel, Zamael, and Zuriel.

Almost all of the archangels have names that end in "-el." *El* means "shining being" or "shining light" in Hebrew. Metatron and Sandalphon are two exceptions.

A Jewish evening prayer mentions all four of the main archangels:

May Michael, the protector of God, stand at my right hand;
And Gabriel, the power of God, stand at my left;

Before me, Uriel, the light of God;
And behind me, Raphael, the healing of God.
And above my head, may there be the abiding presence of God,
the Shekinah.

Michael

Represents: Love, courage, strength, and protection
Element: Fire
Direction: South
Season: Autumn
Color: Red
Zodiac signs: Aries, Leo, and Sagittarius

The name Michael comes from the Hebrew *Mikha'el,* which means "who is like God." Michael is the best known archangel, and is thought to be the archangel closest to God. He is the most important angel in Christianity, Judaism, and Islam. As God's most important warrior angel, Michael fights for everything that is good, moral, and virtuous. He works tirelessly to create a world of peace and harmony.

Michael is considered to be the protector of the Roman Catholic Church, and Catholics frequently call him Saint Michael. Catholics pray to Saint Michael to protect them from evil. In Judaism, Michael is considered to be a special friend and protector of the Jewish people. In the book of Daniel, Michael is referred to as "one of the chief princes" and "the great prince which standeth for the children of thy people" (Daniel 10:13–21). Michael rescued Daniel from the lion's den. Many people believe that Michael will appear whenever the world is in grave danger. As God's warrior angel, Michael is said to have single-handedly killed the 185,000 men in King Sennacherib's army who were threatening to capture Jerusalem in 701 BCE. He did this in just one night. It was Michael who threw Satan out of heaven after the war in heaven (Revelation 12:7–9). Because of these deeds, Michael is usually shown carrying a sword. However, he is sometimes depicted holding the scales of justice or a blue flame of protection.

One of Michael's tasks is to receive immortal souls as they reach Heaven. He weighs them to balance their good and bad deeds (Psalms 62:9; Daniel 5:27).

Michael has parallels in other culturally important texts. The Indian *Rig-Veda* has Indra, the Persian *Denkard* has Vahman, the Babylonian *Enuma Elish* has Marduk, and Apollo is the hero in Homer's "Hymn to Apollo." No matter what name they are known by, these angels have always helped humanity.

Michael was originally thought to be a protective spirit, or possibly a god, in ancient Chaldea. The people needed someone to help them in the constant battle between good and evil, and Michael was the perfect symbol of this.

Rudolf Steiner, the Austrian philosopher and founder of the Anthroposophical Society, believed that Michael had been promoted from an archangel to an archai, and this gave him the freedom and time to help humanity as a whole (Parisen 1990, 118–119).

According to the Gnostics, Michael, along with the other main archangels, was present at the creation of the universe. In the apocryphal Gospel of Bartholomew, Michael collected clay from the four corners of the earth, and God created humans from this. Michael is thought to be the "Angel of the Lord" who stopped Abraham from sacrificing his son Isaac

(Genesis 22:10). According to Jewish legend, Michael also appeared to Moses in the burning bush and rescued Daniel from the lion's den (Exodus 3:2; Ginzberg 1954, 2:303; Daniel 6:22). He is also believed to be the angel who freed Peter from prison (Acts 12: 3–19). In the book of Revelation Michael led God's armies who defeated the forces of Satan (Revelation 12:7–9). According to the book of Adam and Eve, Michael did all he could to help Adam after he was expelled from the Garden of Eden. He taught him how to farm and accompanied him on a visit to heaven in a fiery chariot. When Adam died, Michael persuaded God to allow his soul to enter heaven. Ever since, Michael has accompanied souls up to heaven.

An ancient tradition says that Michael told Sarah, Abraham's wife, that she would bear a son. Michael, Gabriel, and Raphael were temporarily in human form while undertaking a mission for God. Michael's task was to convey the exciting news to Sarah that she would bear a son. Raphael was sent to heal Abraham after his circumcision, and Gabriel's task was to destroy Sodom and Gomorrah. Michael, Raphael, and Gabriel are not mentioned by name in the Biblical account of this meeting (Genesis 18:2–33).

Michael is venerated in France and as Saint Michael is the patron saint of sailors. In 708 CE Michael appeared to Saint Aubert, the bishop of Avranches, and asked him to build a shrine on what is now known as Mont-Saint-Michel. The shrine was ultimately replaced with a church that is fully surrounded by water at full tide.

In Judaism, Michael is believed to be the author of Psalm 85, which discusses the many sufferings of Israel. An old Jewish tradition says that Michael, Gabriel, Raphael, Uriel, and Metatron successfully fought Satan for Moses's body and then buried him. In some traditions, it was Michael who carried the body of Mary, the mother of Jesus, to heaven. Some people believe that Mary didn't die but was carried directly to heaven by Michael. After their captivity, the Jewish people recognized Michael as protector of the Jewish nation.

In Islam, Michael is known as Mikhail. The Koran says that Mikhail shed tears over the sins of the faithful, and cherubim are formed from these. In Islam, Mikhail has a million tongues, each of which can speak a million languages. His long saffron hair reaches down to his feet. Each hair contains a million faces that each contain a million eyes that cry seventy-thousand tears. His beautiful wings are made of green topaz. Mikhail takes his work seriously and never laughs (Redfield 2002, 196).

In the Islamic tradition, another of Michael's tasks is to look after the bell trees in heaven. These are golden trees covered with silver bells. The sound they make is so beautiful and so powerful that any humans who heard it would immediately die. Each bell emits a light that enables the inhabitants of paradise to see things they could never even imagine while living on earth (Kabbani 1995, 170).

The Feast of Michaelmas has been celebrated since the year 530 CE. This feast day was instituted to celebrate the consecration of a new church that had been built near Rome. As Michael is the patron of knights, this feast was an important one during the Middle Ages. Today, Michael's special day is celebrated by Anglicans and Catholics on September 29. In the Greek, Armenian, Russian, and Coptic churches, Michael is celebrated on November 8.

You can ask Michael for help whenever you need guidance, protection, or inspiration to action once you've faced your fears.

Gabriel

Represents: Overcoming doubt and fear, harmony, wisdom, hopes, and wishes

Element: Water

Direction: West

Season: Winter

Color: Emerald

Zodiac signs: Cancer, Scorpio, and Pisces

The name Gabriel means "God is my strength." Gabriel sits on the left-hand side of God, and is considered God's main messenger. An old Jewish legend says that Gabriel introduced himself to Abraham by saying, "I am the angel Gabriel, the messenger of God" (Ginzberg 1909, 1:189).

Depending on the situation, Gabriel has been called a number of names, including Angel of the Annunciation, Angel of Mercy, Angel of Revelation, Chief Ambassador to Humanity, Divine Herald, Prince of Justice, and Trumpeter of the Last Judgment. Gabriel is God's chief messenger. The first time he appeared in the Bible is when he visited Daniel to explain a vision to him (Daniel 8:16).

Gabriel is the angel of purification, guidance, and prophecy. As Gabriel has always been associated with pregnancy and birth, he is also known as the angel of childbirth and of hope. He is often called upon by women who are hoping to conceive. Gabriel was the angel who visited Zacharias and told him that his wife, Elizabeth, would give birth to John the Baptist (Luke 1:5–25). Gabriel also visited Mary and told her that she'd give birth to Jesus (Luke 1:26–35). The greeting that Catholics believe Gabriel said, "Hail Mary," became part of a famous prayer: "Hail Mary, full of grace, the Lord is with you. Blessed are you among women and blessed is the fruit of your womb, Jesus. Holy Mary, Mother of God, pray for us sinners, now and at the hour of our death. Amen." In the Catholic tradition, it was Gabriel who told the shepherds of Jesus's birth (Georgian 1994, 53). The Catholic Church celebrates the Feast of Saint Gabriel on March 24.

In medieval times, the Angelus bell was often known as the Gabriel bell. The Angelus is a Roman Catholic devotion that is recited three times a day, at 6 a.m., noon, and 6 p.m. The bell is rung to honor the Annunciation. The first words of the prayer are "*Angelus Domini nuntiavit Mariae*," which mean "the angel of the Lord brought tidings to Mary."

There are many legends that involve Gabriel. One of the most charming of these says that Gabriel teaches unborn children about heaven. Just before they're born, Gabriel touches them above the upper lip to ensure that they won't remember what he told them until they die. Gabriel's touch forms the philtrum, or cleft, between the nose and the upper lip.

Many Christians believe that it was Gabriel who told the good news about Christ's birth to the shepherds. Gabriel is said to have warned Mary and Joseph that Herod's soldiers were searching for the newborn king. Gabriel is also thought to have rolled away the stone that sealed the tomb of Jesus. In the Christian tradition, Gabriel will blow the horn to wake the dead on Judgment Day.

In Islam, Gabriel is also called Djibril. The religion of Islam began when Djibril visited Muhammad at Mount Hira and told him he was a prophet. Muslims also believe that Djibril dictated the Koran to Muhammad over a period of twenty-three years (Lambert 2013, 287). In the Islamic tradition, Gabriel taught Noah how to build his ark and ordered angels to bring timber from the cedar trees in Lebanon. It took 124 thousand planks to build the ark. The name of a prophet was inscribed on each one. God sent an angel to inspect each plank to make sure it was suitable.

Muslims also believe that Gabriel presented the Black Stone of the Kaaba to Abraham. This stone is kissed by Muslims who make the annual pilgrimage to Mecca.

In the thirteenth century, the Sufi poet Ruzbihan Baqli had a vision in which he saw Gabriel. He explained, "In the first rank I saw Gabriel, like a maiden, or like the Moon among the stars. His hair is like a woman's, falling in long tresses. He wore a red robe embroidered in green ... He is the most beautiful of Angels ... His face is like a red rose" (Baqli 1997, 47).

An ancient Jewish legend involves Gabriel and a lazy angel called Dubbiel, who was the guardian angel of Persia. God had become frustrated with Israel and ordered Gabriel to kill all the Jews by pouring burning coals on them. Any survivors were to be killed by the Babylonians. Gabriel felt sorry for the people of Israel and asked Dubbiel, the laziest angel in heaven, to pass the burning coals to him. Dubbiel was so slow that the coals were almost cold when Gabriel finally threw them at Israel. Gabriel didn't stop there. He spoke to the Babylonians and convinced them that it made more sense to force the Israelites into Babylon than it was to kill them. When God heard about this he was furious and demoted Gabriel from his position as chief minister in heaven. He gave this position to Dubbiel. Dubbiel immediately started helping the Persians at the expense of every other country. Three weeks later, when God was having a meeting with his highest ranking angels, Gabriel came into the room and made an astute comment. God was impressed with this, and immediately restored Gabriel to his former position.

One of the more unusual stories about Gabriel is that he invented coffee. Apparently, Muhammad felt extremely tired one evening and was ready to fall asleep. Gabriel brought him a cup of coffee, and Muhammad gained so much strength from it that he defeated forty horsemen and satisfied forty women.

There's a beautiful Sufi story about Gabriel and Moses. God sent Gabriel and ninety-nine other angels to help Moses reach the necessary state of purity to write the Torah on golden tablets. Each of these angels represented an aspect of God, and they taught him 124 thousand words. Each time Moses learned a new word he was raised to a higher level until he could see nothing but pure white. Once he had reached this state, Gabriel told the other angels to fill Moses with the specific attributes they possessed. Finally, Gabriel taught Moses how to make gold and filled Moses' heart with the knowledge that had to be written on the tablets. Moses then wrote the Torah (Kabbani 1995, 18–19).

In the Jewish tradition Gabriel can speak all the languages of the world, and in a single night he taught Joseph all seventy languages that were spoken in the Tower of Babel. At the time Joseph was a humble slave, but this amazing feat instantly made him the second most important person in the land after Pharaoh (Ginzberg 1909, 2:72).

In Judaism Gabriel is associated with the moon. Gabriel is also associated with the element of water. This means he watches over people who travel over water. As both water and the moon symbolize the emotions, Gabriel is also archangel of the emotions.

According to the Zohar II, 11a–11b, Gabriel is described as being in charge of people's souls. When someone dies, Gabriel receives the person's soul and takes it to its new home, which is determined by how the person lived his or her life. When it's time for the soul to reincarnate again, Gabriel accompanies the spirit back to earth.

My favorite story about Archangel Gabriel was recorded by William Blake, the English artist and poet, in his diary. He had been commissioned to draw an angel but was finding it more difficult than he thought it would be. In frustration he asked, "Who can paint an angel?"

He instantly heard a reply: "Michelangelo could."

William Blake looked around, but there was no one with him. "How do you know?" he asked.

The powerful voice replied, "I know, for I sat with him. I am the Archangel Gabriel."

William Blake was impressed with this reply, but was still suspicious. For all he knew, it might have been an evil spirit pretending to be Gabriel. He asked for some evidence.

"Can an evil spirit do this?" the voice asked. William Blake immediately became aware of a bright shape with large wings.

From it radiated a pure light. As William Blake watched, the angel grew larger and larger, and the roof of Blake's study opened to enable Gabriel to rise up into heaven. In his diary, William Blake wrote that Gabriel then "moved the universe." Unfortunately, he didn't explain what happened, but he wrote that he was convinced he had seen Gabriel (Cortens 2003, 39–40).

You can ask Gabriel for help whenever you need confidence or help in handling your emotions or if you feel anxious. Gabriel will provide guidance, inspiration, and freedom from doubt and fears. Gabriel is willing to help anyone who is experiencing problems with conception, carrying an unborn baby, or concerned about childbirth. Gabriel will also help you express yourself clearly and openly.

Raphael

Represents: Healing, abundance, knowledge, and honesty
Element: Air
Direction: East
Season: Spring
Color: Blue
Zodiac signs: Gemini, Libra, and Aquarius

Raphael is the third most important archangel, after Michael and Gabriel. The name Raphael means "God heals" or "the shining one who heals." Consequently, he is frequently called the "divine physician." When Raphael was asked who he was in the apocryphal Old Testament book of Tobit, he replied, "I am Raphael, one of the seven holy angels, which present the prayers of the saints, and which go in and out before the glory of the Holy One" (12:15).

Raphael is not mentioned by name in the Bible but plays a major role as Tobias's guardian in the book of Tobit. This book tells the story of Tobit, a righteous Israelite who became blind after trying to give proper burials to Jews who'd been killed by Sennacherib's army. Tobit was too tired to return home and went to sleep outdoors. During the night, bird droppings fell on his eyes and made him blind. This affected every aspect of his life, and he prayed to God asking to die.

At the same time, in Medina a young woman named Sarah also prayed for death. A demon called Asmodeus had killed every man she'd married on their wedding night. God orders Raphael to heal Tobit and to free Sarah of the demon.

Tobit asks his son, Tobias, to travel to Medina to collect some money that is owed to him. Because it's far away and dangerous, he tells him to find an honest person to travel with him. He meets a man called Azariah who offers to accompany him. Tobias doesn't know that Azariah is actually Raphael in disguise.

The two men set off on their trip. When they come to a river, Tobias washes his feet in the water. A fish tries to swallow his foot. They catch the fish, and Raphael tells Tobias to cut out the heart, liver, and gallbladder. When they arrive in Medina, Raphael tells Tobias about Sarah. He is entitled to marry her, as they're cousins. Raphael tells Tobias he'd be safe if he burned the heart and liver of the fish on the wedding night, as this would drive away the demon when he came for Tobias. Tobias and Sarah marry, and the smoke from the burning heart and liver send the demon Asmodeus to "upper

Egypt." Raphael follows him there and ties him up to prevent him from causing more mischief. Sarah's father had already prepared a grave for Tobias. When he discovered he was still alive, he filled the grave in and ordered a huge wedding feast. Because of the length of time this took, Tobias asked Raphael to collect the money that was owed to Tobit. Once the celebrations were over, Tobias, Sarah, and Raphael return to Ninevah. When they get there, Raphael tells Tobias to make an ointment from the fish's gallbladder, and to rub it on his father's eyes. He does this, and Tobit's sight is restored. Tobit and Tobias are so grateful that they offered half of their fortune to the guide. He told them, "I am one of the seven angels who stand ready and enter before the glory of God. ... when I was with you I was not acting on my own will, but by the will of God." After this, having healed Tobit and Sarah, Raphael returned to heaven. Because of this story, artists usually portray Raphael as a traveller, carrying a staff and a fish.

Early Christians believed that it was Raphael who appeared to the shepherds by night, bringing them "good tidings of great joy, which shall be for all people," regarding Jesus's birth (Jameson 1895, 1:119).

Because of this, he is considered the head of the guardian angels. Raphael is involved in healing the earth and could be considered the guardian angel of humanity. He is sometimes called the angel of compassion. Many people believe that Raphael was the angel who entered the pond in Bethesda and troubled the water. The first person who entered the pool after this was healed (John 5:2–4). Although not mentioned by name in the Biblical account, Raphael is the most likely angel to perform this miracle.

Raphael is also mentioned several times in the book of Enoch. In the first of these, Michael, Sariel, Raphael, and Gabriel looked down on earth from Heaven, and saw that it "was full of godlessness and violence" (I Enoch 9:1). This is possibly the first mention of the four archangels (Black 1985, 129).

In his role as a healer, Raphael is said to have taken away the pain that Abraham suffered after his circumcision and is the angel who healed Jacob's thigh after his fight with an angel (Genesis 32:24–31). An old Jewish tradition says that he helped Noah learn how to build an ark. Once the flood subsided, Raphael gave him a medical book. This is thought to be the *Sefer Raziel*, the book of the angel Raziel. This book consists mainly of spells that Raziel is said to have given to Adam. Unfortunately, the book disappeared and was assumed lost, until Raphael gave it to Noah. Raphael's healing abilities extend far beyond physical healing. He also performs mental, emotional, and spiritual healing. He can literally heal the wounds of mankind.

Raphael is also credited with helping Solomon build the great temple. Solomon prayed to God, asking for help in building the temple. God gave Raphael a special ring to give to Solomon. The seal on the ring was a pentagram, still one of the most important tools in ceremonial magic. Because of this, many people call Raphael the angel of magic tools and the miracles they can create. The pentagram is also one of the oldest medical symbols, and this is likely to be because of its association with Raphael (Conybeare 1898).

Raphael protects travellers and also heals the wounds of martyrs. According to Jewish legend, he also looks after the Tree of Life in the Garden of Eden.

The Catholic Church used to celebrate Raphael on October 24, but today he is usually celebrated on September 29, which is known as a day of Saint Michael and all angels.

You can ask Raphael for help whenever you need additional vitality and energy or are involved in any creative endeavor. Raphael also provides healing, inspiration, wholeness, and unity. He loves teaching and is willing to help anyone who wants to learn.

Uriel

Represents: Clear thinking, clarity, insight, and peace
Element: Earth
Direction: North
Season: Summer
Color: White
Zodiac signs: Taurus, Virgo, and Capricorn

Uriel is the archangel of prophecy and is the last of the four Angels of the Presence. The name Uriel means "God is my light" or "fire of God." Uriel has many duties. In the book of Adam and Eve, he is called the angel of repentance (xxxii:2). In this role he meets the souls of sinners when they first arrive in heaven. He is also the angel of music. In Jewish legend, it's thought that God sent Uriel to warn Noah of the imminent flood (1 Enoch 10:1–3). Because of this, it's believed that Uriel is in charge of all natural phenomena, including thunder, floods, and earthquakes (1 Enoch 20:2). In fact, many people believe that rainbows are a sign of Uriel's presence. He's also a gifted teacher and taught Seth, Adam's son, about astronomy, time, and Hebrew characters (Joel 1836).

Unlike Michael, Gabriel, and Raphael, Uriel is not mentioned by name in the canonical scriptures, but has appeared in many stories and legends. He holds a special place in the Jewish tradition, as he is believed to have given the Kabbalah to the Jews. In the Kabbalah, Uriel is associated with the middle pillar of the Tree of Life, and with Malkuth, the Kingdom. Malkuth represents the world we live in, and is looked after by Archangel Sandalphon. Uriel and Sandalphon work together to look after the health and well-being of the planet. Consequently, Uriel is sometimes called the Great Archangel of the Earth. Uriel is also thought to be the overseer of hell. According to the *Sibylline Oracles*, Uriel holds the keys to hell and will open the gates to hell on Judgment Day (book 2, lines 280–93). He also taught the Torah to Moses.

Uriel is thought to be the angel who destroyed the hosts of Sennacherib (II Kings 19:35). He may also have been the angel who wrestled with Jacob for a whole night (Genesis 32:24–32).

Uriel taught Ezra that evil has a certain amount of time to run its course. Because Ezra couldn't understand this concept, Uriel enabled him to have seven prophetic dreams to explain what he meant. These dreams covered all of history, including the past and the future. Uriel then helped Ezra understand and interpret the messages in his dreams (Ginzberg 2003, 356–357).

In the apocryphal second book of Esdras, Esdras reproached God for helping Israel's enemies. Uriel was traveling with Esdras at the time and told him that he'd reveal God's reasons after Esdras had weighed fire, measured the wind, and brought back yesterday. Esdras admitted that he could do none of those things. Uriel said that if Esdras knew the fire, wind, and days but could not understand them, how could he possibly understand God's intentions when he did not know him? As soon as he heard this, Esdras fell at Uriel's feet and asked for forgiveness (II Esdras 4:9–35).

Uriel is one of the reprobated angels. Because he wasn't mentioned by name in the Bible, he and several other angels, were demoted at the council in Rome in 745 CE.

In *The Magus*, Francis Barrett, the influential English occultist, wrote that Uriel brought the gift of alchemy to mankind (Barrett 1801, 57). This information probably explains why Uriel is the most invoked of all the archangels.

Dr. John Dee, the scholar and astrologer who predicted the approach of the Spanish Armada and advised Queen Elizabeth I on which date to have her coronation, worked extensively with Uriel. Dr. Dee's diary records that on April 6, 1583, Uriel appeared in Dee's scrying ball to tell him that he had forty days in which to write down the "Book of Secrets." This marked the start of a huge amount of work which ultimately produced the secret and sacred language of the angels, known as the Enochian language. Three centuries later, this language was included as part of the teachings of the Hermetic Order of the Golden Dawn, and today it is still taught in many occult schools.

Artists usually depict Uriel with a scroll in one hand and an open flame burning on the palm of his other hand. This flame symbolizes the "fire of God."

As Uriel's element is Earth, you can ask Uriel for help whenever you need grounding. Uriel provides peace and tranquility, transformation, the gift of prophecy, insight, and prosperity. Uriel can also help you find self-worth and appreciate yourself for the wonderful and unique person you are. Uriel is the angel of the eleventh hour, which means he can be called upon whenever you're in the middle of a major emergency or crisis.

The Other Archangels

Michael, Gabriel, Raphael, and Uriel are generally accepted as being archangels. However, there is considerable disagreement about other members of this order. Many other angels have been called archangels, but the reality is that no one knows exactly which angels belong to this group. Here are twelve angels who have all been classified as archangels by at least one reputable source.

Anael

Anael means "the grace of God." Anael is said to be one of the seven archangels of creation. According to the third book of Enoch, Anael transported Enoch to heaven in a fiery chariot. Anael is named as one of the seven great archangels in *The Hierarchy of Blessed Angels* by Thomas Heywood, which was published in 1635. Rudolf Steiner, the philosopher, author, and founder of anthroposophy, also called Anael one of the seven great archangels. However, Anael is not listed as an archangel in the usual hierarchies of Dionysius the Areopagite, Saint Gregory, or the third book of Enoch.

Anael is said to be the angel who called out these words: "Open ye the gates, that the righteous nation which keepeth the truth may enter in" (Isaiah 26:3).

Anael is one of the planetary angels and is associated with Venus. Consequently, he can be called upon for anything that involves love, romance, sexuality, harmony, and peace. He can also be called upon for help with status, recognition, and long-term careers. Anael also helps people overcome shyness and gain confidence in themselves.

Cassiel

Cassiel helps people learn patience and encourages them to do whatever is necessary to overcome their problems and difficulties. He also helps people gain serenity and peace of mind. Cassiel is the angel of karma and helps people understand the law of cause and effect. Cassiel is the lord of Saturn, a slow-moving planet. It takes Saturn four years to orbit the sun, and it can sometimes take that long for Cassiel to resolve a problem. Fortunately, Raphael is happy to talk to Cassiel and speed up the process.

Cassiel is depicted by artists as a fierce-looking man with a dark beard. He wears a crown and holds an arrow made from a feather. He is usually portrayed sitting on the back of a dragon.

Chamuel

The name Chamuel means "he who seeks God." Chamuel is the archangel of compassion and divine love. Some sources say that Chamuel was the angel who comforted Jesus in the Garden of Gethsemane. However, this angel is usually considered to be Gabriel.

Chamuel rights wrongs, soothes troubled minds, and provides justice. In addition, he can help you find the right partner, and if the relationship doesn't last, he can also help you get over the loss of an important relationship. He can help you forgive others, especially people you considered to be friends and lovers. Chamuel loves helping people deepen their relationships and take them to a new level. Chamuel is also willing to help you express your feelings through some form of creativity, such as writing, painting, and music. As Chamuel's element is earth, the best place to contact him is outdoors, especially in a pleasant environment where you'll be free of interruptions, such as a garden, woodlands, or on top of a hill.

You should call on Chamuel whenever you need more strength, courage, determination, and persistence.

Jeremiel

The name Jeremiel means "God's mercy." Jeremiel is mentioned by name in the book of Esdras and the first book of Enoch. He brings matters that have been hidden out into the open. He is considered an angel of transition, as he encourages people to make positive changes in their lives. There is some confusion about Jeremiel's name in the list of archangels, as it's possible that his name is another name for Remiel or Archangel Uriel.

Jophiel

The name Jophiel means "the beauty of God." Jophiel is thought to have guarded the Tree of Knowledge in the Garden of Eden. According to Jewish legend, it was Jophiel who expelled Adam and Eve from the Garden of Eden. He also taught, guided, and looked after Noah's three sons, Shem, Ham, and Japhet. Jophiel is one of the Angels of the Presence and is thought to be a close friend of Archangel Metatron.

He loves beauty and encourages all forms of creativity. Not surprisingly, he is considered the patron angel of artists.

Metatron

The meaning of the name Metatron is unclear, though it could be "the throne beside the throne of God." Metatron is the most important angel in the Jewish tradition. In the third book of Enoch, Metatron is said to sit on a throne while dispensing justice. He was a scribe while on earth and has continued doing this in Heaven. Not surprisingly, he is thought to be God's secretary. In this role he records all the earthly and celestial activities, including the good and bad deeds of Israel. He is also responsible for the well-being of all mankind. According to legend, Metatron was originally Enoch, Adam's great-great-great-great-grandson who lived for 365 years before God turned him into an angel. It is explained in Genesis that "Enoch walked with God; and he was not, for God took him" (5:23–24). Some of the angels were unhappy when God turned a human into an angel. After God answered their objections, God blessed Enoch with 1,365,000 blessings, and enlarged him until he was almost as big as the world. He has thirty-six pairs of wings and 365,000 eyes, each of them as bright as the sun. Metatron is often called the angel of mankind, as he experienced life as a human. Because of this, he can see both the earthly and heavenly points of view. However, he depends on the innate goodness of people to vitalize his spiritual energy.

The Zohar provides an explanation for why Enoch was chosen to become an angel. Apparently, he was born with the same divine spark of spiritual perfection that Adam had possessed. Adam lost this when he was cast out of Eden. God could not allow someone with this divine spark to remain with other mere mortals. Consequently, he was taken to heaven where his perfection would be appreciated and used (1:37b, 1:56b, 1:223b, 2:179a, 3:83b).

In Jewish belief, Metatron carries all prayers directly to God, passing through nine hundred heavens on the way. However, when prayers are said in Hebrew, Metatron calls upon Sandalphon to help him weave the prayer into a garland of flowers that God can wear on his head. Johann Eisenmenger, the German philosopher, claimed that Metatron was God's angel of death who receives God's orders about which souls will be taken each day. In addition to this, he is said to teach the souls of dead children in heaven.

According to legend, Metatron was the angel who wrestled with Jacob for a whole night. However, several other angels, including Michael and Zadkiel, have also been associated with this event. It's possible that this verse in Exodus refers to Metatron: "Behold, I send an angel before thee, to keep thee in the way and to bring thee unto the place which I have prepared" (23:20).

You can call upon Metatron whenever you need to think deeply or need to build up your self-esteem.

Raguel

Raguel means "friend of God." According to the second book of Enoch, Raguel and Sariel are two of the angels who may have escorted Enoch to heaven. Enoch wrote that Raguel is one of the seven archangels and the one responsible for carrying souls up to heaven. Raguel ensures that all the angels maintain the highest possible standards of behavior. His duties include justice, harmony, discipline, and retribution. He is considered to be God's kind and caring assistant.

In the apocryphal Revelation of John, God calls upon Raguel after separating the sheep from the goats: "Then shall He send the angel Raguel, saying: Go, sound the trumpet for the angels of cold and snow and ice, and bring together every kind of wrath upon those that stand on the left" (*The Ante-Nicene Fathers* 1886, 586).

Raguel, along with Uriel and Samiel, was demoted by Pope Zachary at the council in Rome in 745 CE. In fact, Pope Zachary called Raguel a demon "who passed himself off as a saint." These are harsh words to describe an angel who ensures other angels behave well.

You can ask Raguel for help whenever you have difficulties with others, especially children or young people. Raguel also helps you affirm or strengthen your faith and provides harmony in your life.

Raziel

The name Raziel means "secret of God." Raziel stands behind the curtains in front of the throne of God and is able to see and hear everything that is discussed. He uses what he has learned to reveal to humanity the teachings and decrees of God.

Raziel felt sorry for Adam and Eve when they were expelled from the Garden of Eden and gave Adam the book of Raziel. This book contained all the knowledge of the universe and enabled Adam and Eve to make a life for themselves outside the garden. Jewish legend says that some angels were jealous of all the knowledge Adam had learned from this book, stole it, and threw it into the sea. When God saw how upset Adam was over this loss, he called Rahab, angel of the sea, and asked him to find the book and give it back to Adam. Many years later, this book was found by Enoch, who had a dream telling him where the book was located. With the help of this book, Enoch became the wisest man of his time, and eventually it came into the hands of Noah, who used it to help build his ark. Hundreds of years later, King Solomon used the information in the book to gain wisdom, create magic, and heal others.

Raziel is said to have blue wings and is surrounded by an intense yellow aura. He wears a shimmering, gray robe. Raziel enjoys helping original thinkers formulate their ideas.

You can ask Raziel for help whenever you have a major problem to resolve.

Remiel

The name Remiel means "mercy of God" and "God raises up." This name is perfect, as Remiel's main task is to lead souls up to heaven. He looks after the souls of the faithful after they have been weighed by Michael. Remiel is also called the angel of hope. He helps people who have a special need see into the future. Remiel is sometimes known as the angel of divine vision. In the Apocalypse of Baruch, he tells Baruch of a vision he had about him defeating the forces of Sennacherib. In some accounts Remiel is said to be the angel who destroys the army. (Michael is also sometimes credited with this.) In I Enoch he is said to be one of the seven archangels who attend the throne of God (20:8). It's interesting to note that later, in the same book, Enoch mentions that Remiel was one of the fallen angels.

You can ask Remiel for help whenever you need calm, peace, and harmony in your life.

Sandalphon

Sandalphon (sometimes spelled Sandalfon) is said to be Metatron's twin brother. According to Jewish legend, he was originally the prophet Elijah. The Bible says, "Elijah went up by a whirlwind into heaven" (II Kings 2:11). He is said to be one of the Angels of the Presence. In Jewish tradition he weaves garlands of flowers out of Jewish people's prayers. He then charms them to make them rise and sit on the head of God. Despite his preference for Jewish prayers, Sandalphon is willing to take any prayers to heaven. He is a giant among angels, and his size terrified Moses when he was taken to heaven to receive the Torah. It is said that it would take five hundred years to climb from Sandalphon's feet to the top of his head. Sandalphon is usually depicted with birds flying around him and a sword close by. This is because he looks after all bird life and is also one of God's warrior angels. He works with Michael in their endless battle against Satan. It is Sandalphon who decides whether an unborn baby will be a boy or girl.

Sariel

Sariel means "God's command." Sariel is mentioned three times in the book of Enoch (I Enoch 9:1, 10:1; II Enoch 20:6). This is not surprising, as Sariel and Raguel were two of the angels who may have taken Enoch up to heaven. He or she is the angel responsible for disciplining any angels who behave badly. In some traditions Sariel also helps people who want to learn and is thought to be the angel who taught Moses. He also went to Mount Sinai to retrieve Moses's soul after he died. Apparently, God sent Sariel to Jacob to interpret his dream about the ladder. Sariel also assists Raphael in his ministry of healing and is often called an angel of healing.

An unusual aspect of Sariel is that he sometimes appears in the form of an ox. In the *Falasha Anthology*, a collection of texts and prayers recorded by an ancient Jewish community, he is called both Sariel the trumpeter and Sariel the angel of death. Sariel is commonly invoked in ceremonial magic, and even today some people wear amulets with the name Sariel on them to provide protection against the evil eye.

You can ask Sariel for guidance and help whenever you need to make your life more orderly. Sariel encouraged Moses to study. Consequently, he's willing to help people who want to learn. Both Sariel and Raphael are willing to assist with healing.

Zadkiel

The name Zadkiel means "the righteousness of God." According to the Zohar, one of the most important books of Kabbalah, Zadkiel and Zophiel are Michael's two important companions who help him whenever he rights a wrong or is forced into battle (Zohar, Numbers 154a). In Jewish legend, Zadkiel is best known as being the angel of God who prevented Abraham from sacrificing his son Isaac. However, several other angels, including the most likely contender, Michael, have been credited with doing this.

Dionysius the Areopagite included Zadkiel in his list of seven archangels. Zadkiel is a planetary angel and is associated with Jupiter. Because of this, Zadkiel has always been associated with benevolence, abundance, forgiveness, mercy, tolerance, compassion, prosperity, and good fortune, all qualities associated with this planet.

You can call on Zadkiel when you need more joy and fun in your life. Zadkiel will also help you improve your memory. Zadkiel can be called upon for help with any legal or financial problems.

The Specialist Angels

Over the centuries, literally thousands of angels have been named, and there are countless others who have never been identified. This isn't likely to bother them, as angels exist solely to serve God and have no personal ego.

Every angel has a purpose, no matter where they happen to be in the hierarchy of angels. Some angels with particular skills and interests are called specialist angels, and many of these have been identified. As early humans were fascinated by the stars and the movements of the planets, a large number of these angels have been associated with astrology.

Angels of the Seven Heavens

Christians, Jews, and Muslims all believe in heaven. The concept of seven heavens, rather than just one, is ancient and can be traced back to the ancient Sumerians some seven thousand years ago. The seventh heaven is where God lives, and this is why the expression "to be in seventh heaven" means the person could not be happier. The seven heavens can be visualized as seven concentric circles surrounding the earth.

First Heaven

The first heaven is the physical world, including the stars, planets, clouds, and all natural phenomena. The ruling angel of the first heaven is Gabriel. The angels who live here include the other three main archangels of Michael, Raphael, and Uriel. This is because each of them rules a planet and is consequently associated with the natural phenomena of the universe. Adam and Eve are said to live here, too.

Second Heaven

The second heaven is where sinners wait for Judgment Day. This includes some of the fallen angels who are imprisoned there. Moses visited the second heaven. The ruling angel of the second heaven is Raphael. In the Islamic tradition Jesus Christ and John the Baptist live in the second heaven.

Third Heaven

According to the second book of Enoch, the third heaven contains the two opposites of heaven and hell. The Garden of Eden and the Tree of Life are in the southern half of this heaven, and are said to be guarded by three hundred angels of light. Milk, honey, oil, and wine flow down from four springs into the Garden of Eden. It is here that celestial bees spend their days creating manna, the heavenly nectar that God provided for the Israelites during their time in the desert. God is said to rest here as he ascends up to paradise.

The northern half of the third heaven contains hell, where evildoers are tormented and punished for their transgressions. Some of the fallen angels are in hell.

The ruling angel of the third heaven is Baradiel.

Fourth Heaven

The fourth heaven contains the heavenly Jerusalem, the Holy Temple, and the Altar of God. In some accounts, it also contains the Garden of Eden. The movements of the sun and moon are also looked after from here. The ruling angel of the fourth heaven is Michael.

Fifth Heaven

Some of the fallen angels are confined here (as well as in the second and third heavens). The giant Grigori, or Watchers, are a group of fallen angels who are imprisoned here because they lusted after, and fornicated with, people on earth. They live in the northern part of this heaven. The southern part is the home of vast ministering angels who constantly sing songs of praise to God. According to the prophet Zephaniah, a number of angels from the choir of dominions also live here. Zadkiel is generally considered to be the ruler of the fifth heaven. However, some accounts say that this role is held by Sandalphon.

Sixth Heaven

The celestial records are kept in the sixth heaven, and choirs of angels constantly study them. Seven phoenixes and seven cherubim live here and spend their time praising the Lord. There are two rulers of the sixth heaven. Zebul rules the sixth heaven at night, and Sabath rules during the daytime. The sixth heaven is said to be covered with snow, and the inhabitants are regularly buffeted by powerful storms.

Seventh Heaven

God, the seraphim, the cherubim, and the thrones all live in the seventh heaven. God is said to be surrounded by the four Angels of the Presence: Michael, Gabriel, Uriel, and Penuel. Spirits of people yet to be born are said to live here. The seventh heaven is ruled by Archangel Cassiel (or possibly Michael).

The Planetary Angels

The ancient Romans associated the seven visible planets with the days of the week. Gradually, more and more elements, including angels, became associated with the planets. The first documented evidence of this comes from twelfth-century Spain when European scholars started translating valuable manuscripts from the past. The angel association is not surprising, as people thought each planet contained some sort of intelligence that guided and directed it in its orbit through the heavens. A number of different associations have been made, but the generally accepted ones are as follows:

> *Sunday:* Sun—Michael (also Raphael)
> *Monday:* Moon—Gabriel

Tuesday: Mars—Samael (also Chamuel)

Wednesday: Mercury—Raphael (also Michael)

Thursday: Jupiter—Zadkiel (also Sachiel and Zachariel)

Friday: Venus—Haniel

Saturday: Saturn—Cassiel (also Orifiel and Zaphkiel)

The *Liber Juratus*, sometimes called *The Sworn Book of Honorius*, is a famous thirteenth-century grimoire that influenced magicians for hundreds of years. It gives some indication of the number and variety of angels that have been associated with the planets and days of the week. It lists 47 angels for Sunday, 56 for Monday, 52 for Tuesday, 45 for Wednesday, 37 for Thursday, 47 for Friday, and 50 for Saturday.

Angels of the Zodiac

Angels have been associated with the signs of the zodiac for thousands of years. In Jewish tradition, Masleh is the angel in charge of the zodiac. The angels of the zodiac are frequently petitioned to help in rituals involving the qualities of the specific sign. You can communicate with the angel ruling your horoscope sign whenever you wish. This is especially useful if you're wanting information about your future. If you're making a request for someone else, you should use the angel relating to their zodiac sign. The best time to contact them is on your birthday, but you can call on them whenever you wish.

In *The Book of Secret Things*, Abbot Johannes Trithemius, the German occultist and teacher of Paracelsus, included the following traditional associations of angels with the horoscope signs (Davidson 1967, 342).

Aries: Malahidael or Machidiel

Although Malahidael and Machidiel (God's fullness) appear frequently in angel lore as different angels, it seems likely that they're two names for the same angel.

Machidiel is the angel of March and is responsible for people born under the sign of Aries. You can call on Machidiel whenever you need additional strength and courage to stand up for what you believe is right. In the first book of Enoch he's called Melkejal, the angel who looks after the start of the year.

Machidiel is one of the angels of the Tree of Life and is frequently called upon by men performing love magic to attract a suitable woman. Machidiel helps people gain the necessary courage to express their love to others.

Taurus: Asmodel

Asmodel ("I become") governs the month of April and is responsible for people born under the sign of Taurus. He is often called the angel of patience, and he encourages slow but steady progress. At one time, Asmodel was a cherubim who guarded the entrance to the Garden of Eden. This might explain his love of flowers and nature. Unfortunately, Asmodel was demoted after a major rebellion in heaven. He can be called upon for any matters involving love, romance, and nature. However, he's happiest when he's helping people remain focused on their goals, especially matters that help them steadily improve their financial positions.

Gemini: Ambriel

Ambriel governs the month of May and is responsible for people born under the sign of Gemini. He is a prince of the order of thrones and is often thought to be an archangel. You can call on Ambriel for any matters involving communication. He is concerned about right and wrong and is often depicted with one hand raised in front of him to ward off evil energies. He enjoys helping people who are seeking new opportunities and responsibilities.

Cancer: Muriel

Muriel governs the month of June and is responsible for people born under the sign of Cancer. Muriel is also one of the four regents of the choir of Dominions. Muriel is the angel of peace and harmony. He is willing to help anyone but especially enjoys working with people in close relationships. Muriel also helps people who love nature. You can call on Muriel whenever you need help in controlling your emotions. You can also ask Muriel for help when you're working on developing your intuition.

Leo: Verchiel

Verchiel governs the month of July and is responsible for people born under the sign of Leo. Verchiel is one of the ruling princes in the choir of powers. Some authorities say he's also a prince in the order of virtues. Papus (a pseudonym of Gérard Encausse), the Spanish-born French physician and occultist, claimed Verchiel was governor of the sun.

Verchiel helps people who crave friendship and love. He provides enthusiasm, energy, and a sense of fun. You should also call on Verchiel if you're experiencing problems with family or friends.

Virgo: Hamaliel

Hamaliel governs the month of August and is responsible for people born under the sign of Virgo. He's in charge of the order of virtues. Hamaliel can be invoked for any problems involving logic, clear thinking, and attention to detail. Hamaliel counsels patience, slow but steady progress, cooperation with others, and a practical approach to solving problems.

Libra: Zuriel or Uriel

Zuriel ("my rock is God") governs the month of September and is responsible for people born under the sign of Libra. Zuriel is the prince regent of the order of principalities. Zuriel can be invoked to create harmony and to improve relationships. Zuriel is also the angel of childbirth and is sometimes called upon to help ease the pain the mother is experiencing. A thirteenth-century manuscript, the book of Raziel, advised pregnant women to wear amulets with the name Zuriel inscribed on them to provide protection during pregnancy and childbirth.

Scorpio: Barbiel

Barbiel governs the month of October and is responsible for people born under the sign of Scorpio. Barbiel is a prince of both the order of virtues and the order of archangels. He also has a strong interest in astrology. There appear to be two angels named Barbiel. The second one is a fallen angel who is said to be one of the twenty-eight angels who rule over the mansions of the moon. You can call on Barbiel to heal physical and emotional pain. Barbiel can help you develop your intuition and compassion.

Sagittarius: Advachiel or Adnachiel

Advachiel governs the month of November and is responsible for people born under the sign of Sagittarius. Advachiel (and Phaleg) are the two rulers of the order of angels. Advachiel is often called the angel of independence and enjoys helping people with an adventurous disposition. You can call on Advachiel whenever you need help doing anything that has an element of risk or falls outside your comfort zone.

Capricorn: Hanael

Hanael ("he who sees God" or "glory of God") governs the month of December and is responsible for people born under the sign of Capricorn. Hanael is prince of the order of principalities and prince of the order of Virtues. He is also one of the ten archangels of the Jewish Kabbalah. *The Hierarchy of Blessed Angels* (1635) by Thomas Heywood listed him as one of the seven great archangels. He is sometimes said to be the angel who transported Enoch to heaven. However, this feat is usually credited to Anafiel. Hanael was one of the angels who helped create the world and later became the angel in charge of the second heaven. Hanael is a planetary angel and is considered one of the rulers of Venus. Hanael is often called the angel of joy, love, and harmony. Hanael can be called upon to help in any matters concerning love, home, and family. Hanael can help with emotional healing and with establishing and maintaining harmonious relationships with others.

Aquarius: Cambiel or Gabriel

Cambiel governs the month of January and is responsible for people born under the sign of Aquarius. Cambiel is interested in science and technology. He is willing to help in any matters concerning forward progress, inventions, and anything that is new and progressive.

Pisces: Barchiel

Barchiel ("God's blessings" and "lightning of God"), frequently known as Barakiel, governs the month of February and is responsible for people born under the sign of Pisces. Barchiel is ruler of the second heaven, and is said to be one of the eighteen Rulers of the Earth. He's considered one of the most important angels in heaven, as he's looked after by 496,000 myriads of ministering angels. Barchiel is in charge of lightning. As well as looking after Pisceans, Barchiel helps rule Scorpio. Barchiel is often invoked to help people seeking good luck. Because of this, he's a popular angel for people involved in gambling and games of chance. Barchiel helps people gain a positive outlook on life.

Angels of the Elements

A number of angels are associated with the four ancient elements of fire, air, water, and earth. These angels are also associated with the four directions. In the Revelation of Saint John the Divine, John wrote, "I saw four angels standing on the four corners of the earth, holding the four winds of the earth" (7:1). You already know half of the angels of the elements, as they're the four best-known archangels—Michael, Raphael, Gabriel, and Uriel.

You can call on the angels of the elements for a wide variety of reasons. Usually, you should contact Aral, Chassan, Taliahad, and Phorlakh when you need help in any of these areas. However, when the need is urgent you can petition the archangels as well.

Fire

Direction: South
Archangel: Michael
Angel: Aral

The angels of fire will help you in any matters concerning enthusiasm, change, energy, power, courage, freedom, ambition, drive, motivation, purification, and strength. They can also help you control negative feelings and emotions like anger, egotism, hate, lust, and possessiveness.

Air

Direction: East
Archangel: Raphael
Angel: Chassan

The angels of air are willing to help you in any matters concerning clarity, discrimination, happiness, logic, intellect, the mind, and knowledge. They can also help you control negative feelings and emotions like anxiety, fear, insecurity, and impulsiveness.

Water

Direction: West
Archangel: Gabriel
Angel: Taliahad

The angels of water are willing to help you in any matters involving compassion, sympathy, understanding, dreams, intuition, femininity, sensuality, and sexuality. They can also help you control negative feelings and emotions like jealousy, deceit, hatred, spite, treachery, and backbiting.

Earth
Direction: North
Archangel: Uriel
Angel: Phorlakh

The angels of earth are willing to help you in any matters involving nature, survival, growth, health, well-being, responsibility, substance, and practicality. They can also help you control negative feelings and emotions like laziness, procrastination, greed, melancholy, and stubbornness.

Angels of Prosperity and Abundance

Everyone wants to be prosperous and successful. Not surprisingly, countless prayers are made every day by people requesting abundance in all areas of life. There are a number of angels whose role is to help people achieve more prosperity in life. They're willing to work behind the scenes and provide you with the necessary opportunities to progress in life and achieve your goals. If you're struggling, it might be hard to believe that we live in an abundant world. However, the fruitfulness of nature shows just how bountiful this world is.

Sadly, many people have a strong poverty consciousness. They do this by constantly dwelling on the negative, rather than positive side of life. If your family expressed thoughts along the lines of "money doesn't grow on trees" while you were growing up, the chances are that you might suffer from poverty consciousness. Fortunately, the angels of abundance are willing to help you change your negative thoughts and attitudes and replace them with feelings of abundance and well-being. The following are some of the more important angels of prosperity.

Your Guardian Angel

Your guardian angel wants you to be successful and will do all he can to provide you with abundance in every area of life. After all, he suffers every time you experience stress, strain, and financial hardship. Although he wants to provide help, he cannot do this without input from you. You need to let your guardian angel know what you want and what you're prepared to do to achieve it.

If you've established a close relationship with your guardian angel, you'll be able to discuss anything, including prosperity, in your conversations. Your guardian angel is your most successful angel of prosperity.

Raziel

We discussed Raziel ("secret of God") in chapter 4, as in the Kabbalah he's considered to be an archangel. He's said to be the author of the book of Raziel, in which "all celestial and earthly knowledge is set down." In actuality, this book was written by a medieval writer, possibly Eleazor of Worms.

Raziel is prince of the order of thrones, a member of the cherubim, and a member of the Sarim, the angel princes in heaven. When you call on Raziel for help, he'll use all his knowledge of the universe to help you attain your goals.

Gamaliel

Gamaliel ("recompense of God") is considered a beneficent angel in the Kabbalah and the Gnostic writings. His work involves carrying blessings from God to people who deserve them. These blessings involve money, joy, happiness, and good luck. Gamaliel is also involved with karma and gives people exactly what they deserve. If they've done good deeds, he'll be extremely generous. Because he hands out rewards so frequently, he's considered a munificent abundance angel.

Pathiel

Pathiel ("the opener") has been invoked for thousands of years by people seeking more abundance in their lives. Ancient Jewish mystics invoked him at the end of Sabbath, confident that he would provide them with whatever they desired. Pathiel is an angel of surprises, and may provide you with opportunities for prosperity and abundance in unusual ways. He is likely to provide you with unexpected, unrequested blessings that will help you gain increased happiness as well as prosperity.

Barchiel

Barchiel ("God's blessings") is the angel who looks after February and the zodiac sign of Pisces. He is the angel of luck and good fortune. He's an extremely positive angel and will help you remain happy, as well as focused, while you're working on improving your finances.

Gadiel

Gadiel ("God is my wealth") is one of the most holy and revered angels in heaven. He is prepared to guide you in the right direction and to provide opportunities to slowly but steadily gain wealth and status.

Angels of Healing

Nothing could be more important than healing. In fact, when you consider that healing involves emotional, mental, and spiritual healing, as well as physical healing, almost everyone needs it. You can ask the angels to help heal your pets, too. When you're healing yourself, you'll probably ask your guardian angel for help. Your guardian angel will also help you heal others.

Whenever possible, you should ask for permission before sending healing to someone else. It may sound strange, but some people actually enjoy being ill. They enjoy receiving attention from others. Others may use it as an excuse to lie in bed rather than face the potentially stressful world outside. Obviously, you can't ask for permission if the person is unconscious or you don't know where they are.

Raphael, Archangel of Healing

Raphael is usually the first choice when someone needs healing. After all, the name Raphael means "God heals." He healed Abraham and Jacob, as well as Tobit and Sarah. This makes him a good choice whenever you, a friend, or a family member are suffering any form of pain. Raphael heals all forms of pain. He'll heal the pain of a broken relationship, for instance. He'll also heal the relationship if that's what both parties want.

Michael, Archangel of Strength and Protection

Archangel Michael has a strong interest in healing, too. He is believed to have created a healing spring at Chairotopa near Colossae. People who bathed in the water while invoking the

Blessed Trinity and Michael would be healed (Guiley 1996, 128).

Michael is also credited with eliminating the plague that had decimated Rome. Saint Gregory (later Pope Gregory) led the populace on a three-day procession through the streets of Rome. When they reached the Tomb of Hadrian, Gregory saw a vision of Michael standing on top of the monument. He was casually sheathing a bloodstained sword. This told Gregory that the plague was over. He erected a church on the site and dedicated it to Michael.

Sariel

Like Raphael, Sariel has always been considered one of the main angels of healing. As Sariel was the angel who taught the principles of hygiene to Rabbi Ishmael, he is often invoked to help heal infections as well as illnesses caused by lack of cleanliness or good hygiene.

Your Guardian Angel

You should call on your guardian angel for help with any illness that isn't life threatening. Your guardian angel is prepared to do everything he or she can to help you, and this includes healing.

Your guardian angel will also help you heal others. While you're communicating with your guardian angel, you can ask him or her to contact the other person's guardian angel and express your desire that the person regain his or her physical health.

Mary, the Queen of Angels

Mary, the mother of Jesus, is venerated by members of the Catholic Church who believe she will comfort and heal people who ask for help. One of her most famous appearances occurred close to Lourdes, in southwestern France, in 1858. Between February 11 and July 16, a fourteen-year-old girl called Bernadette Soubirous saw the Virgin Mary fifteen times at a grotto beside a stream close to the town. Twenty thousand people came to witness her final visitation. In 1862, the Catholic Church decided that the visitations were real, and this enabled the cult of Our Lady of Lourdes to proceed. Today, more than three million pilgrims visit the site every year. The Virgin Mary has made at least four other appearances, accompanied by other angels. These occurred in Guadalupe, Mexico, in 1531; Paris, France, in 1830; Knock, Ireland, in 1879; and Fátima, Portugal, in 1917.

You don't need to be a Roman Catholic to call on Mary, Queen of Angels. All you need to do is make a simple, sincere prayer.

Hodson's Angels of Healing

When I was a teenager, I was fortunate enough to attend many lectures by Geoffrey Hodson (1886–1983), a well-known author, mystic, and Theosophist. He wrote many books, including several on angels. These were based on conversations he had with an angel called Bethelda who visited him in 1924 while he and his wife were resting on a hill overlooking a beech forest in Gloucestershire, England.

Bethelda told him that all the angels were divided into seven categories:

1. *Angels of Power:* These angels help people develop spiritually.

2. *Angels of Healing:* The angels in this group help people maintain good health. They also help people regain their health when they become ill.

3. *Guardian Angels of the Home:* These angels protect every home.

4. *Building Angels:* The angels in this group motivate and inspire us to achieve all that we can in the areas of mind, body, and spirit.

5. *Angels of Nature:* The angels in this group are devas, or elemental spirits, that live in fire, earth, air, and water.

6. *Angels of Music:* These angels sing God's praises and inspire people to sing and worship God.

7. *Angels of Beauty and Art:* These angels inspire people involved in any form of creativity. They also enable people to recognize and appreciate beauty in all its forms.

The angels of healing can be called upon whenever any sort of healing is required. They work under the guidance of Archangel Raphael and provide healing and comfort to people who are unwell. They also provide love and consolation to the bereaved. Bethelda told Geoffrey Hodson that the healing angels struggle to help humanity, as so many people have closed hearts and minds, and this makes it hard to heal them.

Enochian Angels

Dr. John Dee and his scryer, Edward Kelley, recorded a large number of communications from the angelic kingdom between 1581 and 1587. Most of this information was communicated in the Enochian language, and the angels are known as Enochian Angels. Most of the messages came from the Great Angel Ave. However, there were many others, including a female angel called I AM who did not communicate with Dr. Dee directly but sent messages through her children. One of these was an angel named Madimi who appeared as a young girl with golden hair. Madimi's messages captivated Dr. Dee, and he named one of his daughters after her.

The Enochian system has angels of the four directions, which are symbolized as watchtowers. Each watchtower is governed by six Elders, and below them is a huge hierarchy of archangels and angels. The Enochian system is highly involved and complex. Today, four hundred years after Dr. Dee and Edward Kelley recorded the information, more people than ever before are studying the Enochian angels.

six

How to Communicate with Angels

M any people experience angels unexpectedly, often in times of major stress. Several years ago, I met a woman who told me how she and her daughter were saved by an angel. Doreen had just gone to bed when her teenage daughter phoned and asked her to come and pick her up. A fight had broken out at the party she and a friend had gone to, and they were frightened. The party was several miles away, and it was a cold, wet night. Doreen got into her car and drove as fast as she could to collect the two scared girls. Halfway there, the traffic lights ahead of her changed. She jammed on the brakes and the car slid sideways and hit a power pole. There was no one around. After taking several, slow deep breaths,

Doreen got out of the car to see what damage she'd done to her car and the power pole. The power pole was fine, but the front passenger door and the hood of her car looked badly damaged. Doreen got back into her car and tried to start it, but nothing happened. In her haste, Doreen had forgotten to bring her cell phone. She realized that she was totally alone on a horrible night, and anything could be happening to her daughter. As she realized the full extent of her predicament, she started to cry. Suddenly, she heard two gentle taps on the window. She turned and saw a smiling man waving to her. He was holding a flashlight. Instinctively, she felt she could trust him. "You'll need some work done on your car," the man said. "But I might be able to get it going again. Shall I try?"

Doreen wiped away a tear and nodded. The man lifted the hood and spent a few minutes peering at the engine. He made a few adjustments, and asked Doreen to try to start the car again. To her amazement, the car started. She turned to thank the man, but he'd disappeared. She got out of the car, but there was no sign of him or his flashlight. Doreen continued on her journey, found the two terrified girls, and brought them home. The next day, she drove her car to her mechanic who found it hard to believe she'd been able to drive it, as it was so badly damaged.

Doreen believes the mysterious stranger who came to her aid was an angel. Up until that moment, she'd scarcely thought about angels, but the experience changed her life. "How could it not?" she told me. "I was in a terrible situation, and he saved me."

Fortunately, most people don't need to find themselves in a difficult situation to contact angels. There are many ways to communicate with angels. As everyone is different, some methods work better for some people than they do for others. You should experiment with as many different methods as possible and see which ones work best for you. The angels will be thrilled to know you're trying to contact them and will be keen to respond.

How to Gain Angel Awareness

The easiest way to become aware of the angelic kingdom is to allow yourself to become as relaxed as possible, call on the angels, and wait for a response.

Find a quiet place where you're unlikely to be disturbed. I prefer to do this exercise indoors, as I want to avoid any possible distractions. Tell everyone in the house that you don't want to be disturbed for about thirty minutes. Turn off your phone and pull the curtains. You need to be as comfortable as possible. Make sure the room is warm enough and that you're wearing loose-fitting clothes. I like to sit in a recliner chair but sometimes lie flat on the floor. I prefer not to lie on a bed as I fall asleep far too easily.

Once you're ready, close your eyes and take ten slow, deep breaths. Hold each inhalation for a couple of seconds, and exhale slowly. I usually say to myself, "Relax, relax, relax," as I exhale.

Once you've done this, consciously relax every part of your body, starting with your toes and working your way up to the top of your head. This is covered in more detail in chapter 3. Here is another method I use to become completely relaxed:

Make yourself comfortable, close your eyes, and imagine yourself standing on a bluff overlooking a beach and the ocean. You can either remember a time when you actually did this, or you can create the picture in your mind. Imagine the scent and feel of the salt spray, the sound of seagulls overhead, the gentle breeze on your face, and anything else that you can remember or visualize. Some people can visualize everything as a picture in their mind. Others get a sense of it, hear the sounds, or sense the smells. It makes no difference how you "see" it.

Once the scene is clear in your mind, imagine a set of stairs leading down to the beach. My stairs have ten steps, but yours can have as many or as few as you wish. Place your hand on the handrail, and take one step down the stairs. Silently say "ten" as you do this. Visualize yourself doubling your relaxation as you say "ten." Repeat and count down with all of the steps until you're standing on the sand. You should feel totally relaxed after doing this, but to make sure this is the case, visualize giant magnets under the sand that pull out every last vestige of strain or tension in your body. Lie down on the sand feeling totally relaxed and contented.

In this nice, calm, peaceful state, think of your desire to contact the angelic realms. If you wish to speak to a specific angel, think of him or her now. If you have no particular angel in mind, think of your guardian angel. Thank your guardian angel (or the angel you want to communicate with) for looking after you and for his advice and support. Tell your guardian angel that you'd like to be in regular contact, and ask if this is possible. Pause, enjoy the pleasant relaxation in every cell of your body, and wait expectantly.

It's unlikely that you'll receive a response the first time you do this exercise. However, it can happen. I know several people who've made contact on their first attempt. If you're fortunate enough to be one of these, express your love and thanks to your guardian angel or the angel you wish to communicate with. You can then ask for help or advice.

You don't need to feel disappointed if you don't make contact on the first, or even tenth, attempt. You've managed to live successfully on this planet for your entire life without even trying to make contact. The angel you're trying to communicate with may simply be testing you to see how persistent and determined you are. Once you've demonstrated your genuineness and sincerity, he or she will reply to your request.

The response may not come in the way you expect. You may hear a quiet, small voice inside your head. This is immediately recognizable and is quite unlike the constant chatter that goes on ceaselessly inside our heads. The angel's voice will be more powerful and vibrant and will give you knowledge and information that you wouldn't otherwise know.

The response may come in the form of a dream. As dreams fade quickly, you might find it helpful to keep a dream diary beside your bed and record everything you can remember about the dream as soon as you wake up. It's not always easy to determine if your dream came from the angel you were trying to contact or from your subconscious mind. However, with time and experience, you'll realize the insights and messages from your angel are of a higher quality than your thoughts usually are.

You may receive a reply in a completely different way. White feathers are a good example. The interesting thing about white feathers is that once you've received one, you'll notice more and more of them until you finally respond to them. This is particularly the case if you know the angels are encouraging you to do something that you know you should do but don't really want to. I've experienced that on more than one occasion.

A woman I know told me that she experiences a beautiful scent that tells her contact has been made. Although she's tried, she's never managed to find this perfume anywhere else or at any other time. You might start finding small coins or other small objects that alert you to an angelic presence. Some people hear strange sounds, such as someone whistling, that tells them they'll shortly enjoy the company of angels.

A relatively frequent form of communication occurs when a problem or difficulty is suddenly resolved. This usually means that the angel has resolved the problem to everyone's satisfaction.

After making contact with your angel, you should aim to keep the lines of communication open. Initially, this is best done with regular relaxation sessions. However, once you've become accustomed to this, you'll find that you can use odd spare minutes in the course of your day to communicate with your angel. You can enjoy a conversation with your angel while taking a shower, traveling on a bus or train, stuck in traffic, waiting in line, or enjoying a walk. Before going to sleep can be a good time to do this, too, as the communication might extend into your dreams. Any spare time can be put to good use by doing this. With practice, extraneous noise won't bother you. I've had angelic conversations in the middle of crowded airports just after a flight was canceled. Once a good connection has been established, you can contact the angelic realms whenever you wish.

Writing a Letter

Writing a letter to a specific angel is an extremely good way to make contact. It takes time and thought to write a good letter, and this forces you to think about your concern in depth before putting pen to paper. The concentration involved in the process often means that angelic contact is made before you finish writing the letter.

I like to use good-quality paper and a fountain pen. This helps me approach the letter writing in a different state of mine than if I'd scribbled a few lines on a scrap of paper.

You need to take the letter writing seriously, but this doesn't mean you should write in a stiff and formal manner. You wouldn't do that if you were writing to a good friend, and the same thing applies here. Write in a casual, familiar, and friendly manner to achieve the best results.

Obviously, you'll be writing the letter for a specific purpose, and this needs to be explained in as much detail as possible. You might be writing to ask for help for yourself or for someone close to you. Your problems and concerns will be put into proper perspective by writing them down. Of course, the letter might not be related to a problem or difficulty. It could be as simple as asking the angel for a closer connection.

In addition to this, you should tell the angel what's going on in your life. Write about the good things as well as the bad. Write about your family and what they're doing. Write about your hopes and dreams. The process of recording them enables you to clarify them in your mind, and often this turns them into goals that you can pursue.

You'll be amazed at what you produce when you sit down to write a letter to a good friend, which is what your angel is. Most letters of this sort will be written to your guardian angel, and you can use these letters as opportunities to update him or her on what's happening in your life. If you're writing to a specific angel for a particular purpose, you should start by introducing yourself and telling the angel something about you and your life before starting to write about your need for help.

At the end of your letter, you need to thank the angel for reading it and express your hope that he'll be willing to help. Finally, express your love and sign the letter. Seal the letter in an envelope and write "To My Guardian Angel" (or whatever angel you're writing to) on the front.

Once you've written the letter you need to send it to the specific angel. You'll need several minutes of peace and quiet to do this. Sit in front of a lit candle. Rest the back of your right hand on the palm of your left hand, with your left thumb resting on your right palm. (If you're left-handed, you might prefer to rest your left hand on your right palm.) Your letter should be resting on your right palm, held in position by your left thumb.

Gaze at the candle flame, and think about the angel you've written the letter to. If it's your guardian angel, you might think about everything he or she does for you and say thank you. If it's an angel you're contacting for a specific purpose, think about what you know about this angel, and your reasons for contacting him or her. Thank this angel for looking into your concern. Take as long as you need with this part of the process. You may feel the angel's presence. If this occurs, you can immediately enter into a silent communication with him or her. It's more likely that you'll feel a sense of love and protection enfolding you.

When the time seems right, burn the envelope in the candle flame and watch the smoke carrying your message up to your angel. Say a final "thank you" as the smoke is still rising. Once the letter has completely disappeared, get up and carry on with your day, confident that your letter has been delivered.

You should always take great care when using candles. Whenever possible, I place them on metal trays and always have a jug of water handy, just in case of an accident. I've never had any problems but would rather be safe than sorry.

Angel Journal

I enjoy writing in my angel journal and am sure you'll find it helpful, and possibly addictive, if you start your own journal. You'll gain angelic insight while writing in it, and when you reread earlier journal entries, you'll find many good ideas that you'd somehow overlooked before. The journal will also become a record of your spiritual growth and development. As your angel journal is a special private diary, you can record things in it that you'd never dream of telling anyone else. In fact, I've never shown my angel diaries to anyone.

You can write anything you want in your angel diary. You might write to specific angels on particular days. If you're writing an entry on Monday, for instance, you might write a message to Archangel Michael, as he looks after Monday. If you happen to be writing an entry when the sun is in Leo, you might write to Verchiel, who looks after people born under this sign. You don't have to be a Leo to do this. You might also decide to write to the angels of the elements, the angels of the week, or angels that relate to specific concerns and problems. You don't have to wait for a specific day to talk with an angel. If you have an important meeting on Thursday, for instance, you might write a message to the angels who look after Thursday (Sachiel, Zadkiel, and Zachariel) a few days beforehand, asking for help and guidance in the upcoming meeting. If you have nothing specific to write about, you might write a message to the angel of the day thanking him or her for protecting and guiding you. Of course, there's no need to write anything if you've nothing to say. I usually write something, even if it's simply a thanks to the angel of the day.

You don't need to censor yourself or hold back in any way while writing in your journal. If you feel upset or worried about something, express your feelings on paper. Once you've got the concerns out of the way, you can start writing a message to an angel.

You'll probably find that it's easier to write in your journal on some days than on others. Sometimes I've written for an hour or more and wondered where the time went. I love these occasions, as when I read back what I've written, I find the message has been written through me, rather than by me. This means an angel has taken control of my pen and written me a message.

You can write your journal in anything you wish. My first journal was a school exercise book. Since then I've used attractive cloth-bound books that can be bought at stationery stores or online.

I write my journal with a black ballpoint pen. I used one for my very first journal and have continued using it ever since. It might seem strange that I write letters to the angels with a fountain pen yet use a ballpoint pen for my journal. I can't really explain this, except that it's become a habit, and they each seem right for their specific function. Incidentally, I don't use these fountain or ballpoint pens for any purpose other than communicating with angels.

Candle Meditation

This is a particularly good way to make angelic contact. You can do it whenever you wish. I like to do it in the evening with the candle as the only source of light. You can use any candles you wish, but they must appeal to you and feel appropriate for the occasion. I wouldn't use a candle in the shape of a cartoon character, for instance. I love candles and have a large selection of different colored ones to choose from. Sometimes I choose a candle by selecting one that feels right, while at other times I choose a candle based on its color. Each color has a variety of associations attached to it.

Red provides confidence, vitality, enthusiasm, and passion.

Orange provides motivation and also eliminates fears, doubts, and worries.

Yellow stimulates the mind and encourages honest communication.

Green provides stability, contentment, and harmony. It also relieves stress and anger.

Blue promotes loyalty, seriousness, and decision making. It prevents indecision.

Indigo provides faith and helps resolve family problems.

Violet provides inner peace and nurtures the soul.

White promotes peace, stability, close relationships, and reverence.

Pink helps overcome emotional problems and helps you give and receive love.

Gray promotes modesty, reliability, and practicality.

Silver provides confidence, calmness, and good self-esteem.

Gold eliminates negative thoughts about money and worldly success and provides motivation.

White candles can be used for any purpose. Consequently, whenever you feel unsure about what color to use, choose a white one.

You'll need a candle, a table, and a straight-backed chair for the meditation. Place a lit candle on the table about six feet in front of where you'll be sitting. When you sit down, the flame of the candle should be at the level of your forehead and third eye.

Sit down and take a few slow, deep breaths while gazing into the candle flame. Blink when necessary, but resist any temptation to close your eyes. You'll find this occurs frequently, as the process is extremely relaxing. Continue gazing into the flame and think about your desire to contact a specific angel. After a few minutes, you might sense an angelic presence all around you. It's likely to be a sense of calm, warmth, and total tranquility. If you're extremely fortunate, you may even get a glimpse of your angel out of the corner of your eye.

Once you sense that you've made angelic contact, start talking, silently or out loud, to your angel. I prefer to speak out loud, but this is not always possible when other people are within earshot.

Circle of Joy

The circle of joy is similar to a magic circle. It's a special, sacred space that you can work within when doing any type of spiritual work. You can create a circle of joy anywhere that there's enough room. In the summer months, I create a circle of joy outdoors, and I work indoors for the rest of the year.

The circle can be a real circle created by a length of rope, drawn with a piece of chalk, or marked with small objects, such as crystals, stones, ornaments, or candles. I think it's better to start with a physical circle, but with practice, you'll be able to visualize a circle several feet in diameter surrounding you and work within that. When I work indoors, I often use a large circular rug to define the circle of joy. Sometimes I'll visualize a circle, but most of the time I create one using crystals.

Once you've created your circle, you need to turn it into a sacred space. Place a comfortable chair in the middle of the circle. Walk around the circle three or four times and then sit down on the chair. Make yourself comfortable, close your eyes, and take several slow, deep breaths. Imagine a beautiful white light descending from the sky and filling your circle with love and protection. You'll always feel safe and protected whenever you're inside your circle. You'll also be filled with divine love. Once you've created your first circle of joy, you'll find you can create one quickly and easily, no matter where you happen to be.

You can use this circle to relax, to meditate, to think about what's going on in your life, and to talk with the angels.

When you feel ready, ask the angel you wish to communicate with to join you in the circle. Sit quietly and focus on your breathing until you feel the angel has arrived. If you've already communicated with your guardian angel, you'll know instantly when he or she arrives, as you'll sense a change in the energy inside the circle. If you're wanting to talk with an angel you haven't met before, be patient and wait until you receive a sign that he or she is there. You may feel a slight touch on your arm or shoulder. You could sense a change in the temperature of the room. You might even hear a slight sound. It might just be a feeling that he or she is there with you. Whatever occurs, know it comes from the angel you're wanting to communicate with.

Exchange greetings and thank your angel for responding to your request. After you've done that and you feel relaxed in the company of the angel, you can discuss anything you need to know. Once you've finished your conversation, thank the angel sincerely and sit quietly in your circle for another minute or two. When you feel ready, open your eyes, stand, stretch, and leave the circle.

I like to leave the circle in place for a while before packing everything away. Sometimes that's not possible, and I have to dismantle it right away. If you set up your circle in the same place every time, you'll find the area gains more and more spiritual energy each time you create it.

Circle of Protection

The circle of protection uses the circle of joy magic circle along with the four great archangels—Raphael, Michael, Gabriel, and Uriel—to create a powerful ritual of protection. You should master the circle of joy before experimenting with the circle of protection.

Create the circle in the usual way. Walk around it three or four times, but don't enter it yet. Instead have a shower or bath to symbolically purify yourself. Put on loose-fitting, clean clothes, and only then walk into the center of your circle. Face east, close your eyes, and visualize a stream of white light coming down from the heavens and filling your circle with divine love and protection. Wait until you sense that your circle is completely filled with white light and say "thank you" out loud.

Open your eyes and visualize the great archangel Raphael standing in front of you. You might see him the way he usually appears in paintings: as a bearded, robed figure, holding a staff and a fish. It's more likely that you'll see him as a ball of energy or a rainbow of color. Don't worry about how you see or sense Raphael, just as long as you know he's standing right in front of you. When you first start working with this ritual, you might have to imagine he's there. Once you sense that Raphael is there, extend your right hand, with the first two fingers extended, as if you're pointing directly at Raphael. Start at the bottom left-hand side and create an imaginary pentagram (a five-sided star) in the air in front of you. After you've done this, bring your hand back a few inches, and then make a stabbing motion through the center of your pentagram.

Keep your right hand extended as you turn ninety degrees to face south. Visualize the great archangel Michael standing directly in front of you. You may see him as a bearded figure holding a set of scales. He might be in armor with one foot resting on a defeated dragon. He might appear as swirls of color. It doesn't matter how you visualize him as long as you know he's standing right in front of you. Make the sign of the pentagram again and finish with a stabbing motion into the center of the pentagram.

Turn another ninety degrees to face west. This time visualize Archangel Gabriel. Once you've done that, draw another pentagram and make a stabbing motion through it. Finally, turn another ninety degrees and visualize Archangel Uriel in the north. Once you've visualized him completely, create a final pentagram, stab it, and turn to face the east again.

This means you are now totally encircled by the four great archangels and are completely protected. You can do anything you wish inside your circle. You should talk to the archangels and thank them for their help and protection. You might call on any angel you wish to communicate with and enjoy conversing with him or her. You might pray or simply meditate inside your special sacred space.

When you feel ready to close your circle, turn to the east and thank Raphael for his help and protection. Turn to the south and thank Michael, followed by Gabriel and Uriel. When you feel ready, step outside the circle.

I like to have something to eat and drink before carrying on with my day. You'll find this ritual will give you unlimited energy as well as a sense of peace and protection.

Moon Ritual

People have been fascinated with the stars and planets for thousands of years. This fascination still exists. Huge numbers of people watch solar eclipses, the approaches of comets, and anything else that's slightly unusual in the night sky.

The moon, in particular, is an endless source of interest as it waxes (grows) and wanes. Not surprisingly, magicians make use of this when performing their magic. Spells that are intended to create abundance or to make something grow are usually made when the moon is waxing. Likewise, spells designed to eliminate something or remove negativity are performed when the moon is waning.

Unlike the sun, the moon can only be seen by reflected light, rather than its own light. Consequently, it's associated with emotions, feelings, and intuitions—in fact, anything that can be kept hidden and secret. As the moon is nurturing, it's related to mothers, teachers, and other caregivers. It provides inner healing that can release negativity and other problems that are hard to resolve.

Because of this, the moon can be extremely helpful when you need to consult a particular angel. This ritual should be performed at night when the moon is visible, or when you're holding something that relates to the moon. As the moon's metal is silver, anything silver can be associated with the moon. The moon also relates to gemstones that are white, such as moonstones, opals, clear and white beryl, and diamonds. It is also connected to stones that come from the ocean, such as pearls and coral, or are the color of the sea, such as aquamarine, which is the blue variety of beryl.

Lavender and clary sage are scents that relate to the moon, and they can also be used in a moon ritual, if you wish.

Finally, Monday is the moon's day and is the best day to perform this ritual.

Ahead of time, think about your need to contact a particular angel. If the need involves attracting anything to you, any form of increase, or matters concerning healing and fertility, you should perform the ritual when the moon is waxing. If your need involves severing ties, endings, or eliminating something from your life, perform this ritual when the moon is waning. Even though this ritual sometimes involves eliminating something from your life, you can't ask the angel to do anything that is underhanded or could hurt another person. Remember, you can't completely sever ties with a family member, either. There are karmic reasons for this.

Start by creating a magic circle somewhere that is illuminated by the light of the moon. Place a chair in the center, facing the moon. (If the moon isn't visible, sit indoors and hold a gemstone or something made from silver.) Gaze at the moon and take several slow, deep breaths to relax your body and mind. When you feel sufficiently relaxed, close your eyes, and think of your need to contact a particular angel. At this stage, you might perform the circle of protection and surround yourself with all four major archangels. Alternatively, you might call on Gabriel for protection. Gabriel is the archangel who relates to the moon.

Once you feel safe and protected and are aware of the presence of Gabriel, say a brief prayer that explains your need. Call on the angel you require and ask him to come to you. You might feel a slight sensation, such as a gentle breeze, a slight touch, or a trace of perfume. Be patient. It might take several minutes for your angel to appear. When he does, thank him for coming to your aid, and tell him everything you can that relates to your problem. Finally, ask him to help you resolve it. Wait for his response. No matter what the answer happens to be, thank the angel for coming to your aid, ask if you can call on him again, and say goodbye. Focus on your breathing for about thirty seconds, and then thank Gabriel (and the other archangels if you're doing this inside the circle of protection). Finally, look up at the moon and thank it for helping you, too.

Leave the circle and eat and drink something. I usually eat a handful of nuts and raisins and drink a glass of water.

Communicating with a Pendulum

A pendulum is a small weight attached to a length of thread or chain. They come in a wide variety of shapes and sizes, and are easily obtainable from New Age stores and online. You can even make your own pendulum by attaching a key, ring, or piece of crystal to several inches of thread. The weight needs to be heavy enough to keep the thread taut when you hold it. Three ounces is perfect. I have a small greenstone pendant that a friend made for me. I wear it around my neck as a protective amulet and use it as a pendulum whenever I'm out and about and don't have a regular pendulum with me.

Start by holding the pendulum near the end of the thread, with the weight suspended an inch or two above the surface of a table. Use your right hand if you're right-handed or your left if you're left-handed. Rest the elbow of this hand on the table, and hold the thread between your thumb and first finger. Start by gently swinging the pendulum from side to side. Follow this by swinging it in different directions, and also rotate it in clockwise and counterclockwise directions. Experiment by holding the thread or chain in different places to create a longer or shorter length.

Once you've become familiar with the different movements of the pendulum, stop it with your free hand. Ask your pendulum, "Which movement indicates yes?" You can ask the question silently or out loud. Keep the hand that's holding the pendulum as still as possible, and wait for a response. If you haven't used a pendulum before, it might take a few minutes to move. Allow the pendulum to move until it's indicating a particular direction. It might move backward and forward, swaying toward and away from you. It might move from side to side, or it might move in circles, either clockwise or counterclockwise. The movements are unlikely to be large when you first experiment with this, but you'll find the movements will become stronger with practice.

Once you've determined which movement indicates yes, ask it to indicate the no direction. Follow this with "I don't know," and "I don't want to answer." Make a note of the different movements. It pays to ask these four questions every now and again, especially if you haven't used the pendulum for a while. It doesn't happen often, but sometimes the movements can change.

Now you can ask the pendulum any questions you wish, as long as they can be answered by the four possible responses. Start by asking your pendulum questions that you can either confirm afterward or already know. You might, for instance, ask, "Is my name (so and so)?" If you've given your correct name, you should receive a positive response. Likewise, you might ask, "Am I male?" If you are, the pendulum should give a positive response. If you aren't, it will give a negative response. You could follow this by asking questions about your work, marital status, number of children, and so on. The purpose of these initial questions is to enable you to become familiar and comfortable with the movements of the pendulum.

However, you shouldn't ask the pendulum questions that you are emotionally involved with. For instance, if you already have three sons and were pregnant and hoping for a daughter, you'd probably ask the pendulum, "Will I have a girl?" In this case, the pendulum will give you the answer you want to hear because your mind can overrule the movements of the pendulum. In a situation like this, you should ask someone with no emotional involvement in the answer to ask the pendulum for you.

You'll find the pendulum extremely useful in everyday life. If you lose your car keys, for instance, you can use your pendulum to find them. Start by asking if the keys are inside your house. If the pendulum says yes, ask if the keys are in, say, the living room, and continue doing this until it says yes again. If necessary, you can then ask the pendulum about different parts of the room until you locate your keys.

You can also use your pendulum to communicate with the angelic realms. I have a beautiful crystal pendulum that I use only for angelic communication. This is because angels respond well to crystal, and it doesn't seem appropriate to use the same pendulum I use for mundane purposes for communicating with angels. Any crystal will work well for this. My favorite crystal is selenite, which is a translucent white crystal. It is a protective crystal that has a special association with Gabriel. I also have a few pendulums that have celestite crystals as the weight. Celestite helps you receive angelic messages as thoughts in your head. I also possess several pendulums that are made from rutilated quartz. Rutilated quartz is commonly known as "angel hair," as it looks as if strands of hair are trapped inside the crystal. Quartz amplifies your angelic communications, making it easier to send and receive messages.

If you wish, you can ask the angels to help whenever you're dowsing with a crystal. All you need do is ask, "Do I have the angels' blessing on the questions I'm about to ask?" If you receive a positive response to this, you can proceed knowing that angels are surrounding you and will provide you with help and support.

Most of the time, you'll receive a positive response when you ask the angels to help you. However, you'll occasionally receive a negative response to this question. When this occurs, you need to look closely at the questions you were going to ask to make sure that they're helpful for everyone involved. Another possibility is that the angels think you'll be able to discover the answer on your own, without the need of a pendulum. Some people use the pendulum as a crutch and use it all the time. I almost always have a pendulum with me ready for use. As I use it only when I can't find the answer any other way, it's common for me not to use it for several weeks and then possibly use it three or four times in a single week.

You'll find your pendulum extremely useful when communicating with your guardian angel. Set aside enough time to enjoy a worthwhile conversation with your guardian angel. I find it helpful to make a list of the matters I wish to discuss ahead of time. I prefer to have these conversations in the evening, as I like to have a white candle on the table I'm using and use it for illumination. Ask your guardian angel if he or she is available for a conversation. Almost always, you'll receive a positive response and will be able to immediately communicate using your pendulum. Occasionally, your guardian angel may be busy with another task or may feel the time is not right for you. This is especially the case if you're angry, upset, anxious, or stressed. Even if you have no idea why your guardian angel is not available, accept it in good grace and try again later.

If your guardian angel hasn't told you his or her name, you can use your pendulum to learn what it is. All you need do is go through the alphabet one letter at a time asking your angel each time if it happens to be the first letter in his or her name. You need to repeat this as many times as necessary to determine the full name.

Once you've made contact with your guardian angel you can ask him or her anything you wish, as long as you phrase the questions in such a way that they can be answered with yes, no, "I don't know," and "I don't want to answer" responses.

Walking with an Angel

I've left my favorite method of making contact with an angel until last. I go for a walk almost every day. I leave my cell phone at home and enjoy having time to think while getting some exercise at the same time. Although it looks as if I'm walking by myself, frequently I'll invite an angel to walk with me. This is usually my guardian angel, but on occasions I'll ask other angels to join me.

I start my walk in the usual way. After about five minutes, I'll ask an angel if he or she would like to walk with me. I continue walking, and after a minute or two, I'll become aware that the angel I called on is walking with me. I won't see or hear the angel but will have a strong sense that he or she is beside me. Once I'm aware of this, I'll start talking with him or her. As I usually walk along suburban streets, I've discovered that it's best to do this silently rather than out loud. The angel's replies appear as thoughts in my mind.

One of the things I particularly enjoy about this form of angelic communication is that we can indulge in some small talk before going into whatever my concerns happen to be. I don't want to waste any angel's time and would never contact an angel purely for a chat. Consequently, there's always something that I'd like to discuss, but some small talk first makes the conversation feel like a good talk between two close friends.

Once the conversation is over, I thank the angel, say goodbye, and finish the walk on my own.

Once you've gained experience at talking to an angel this way, you'll find that you can do it anywhere, even in a crowded shopping mall or traveling in rush-hour traffic.

Feathers

White feathers are a traditional way of sensing angels. I always enjoy finding a white feather, as it reminds me that we're constantly surrounded by angels. Feathers can also be a sign that angels are wanting to communicate with you. About twenty years ago, I wrote a book called *Spirit Guides & Angel Guardians*. At the time, I had no intention of writing anything else on the subject. However, the thought of writing a book, or series of books, on the major archangels kept popping into my mind. I kept dismissing the thought until I found an angel feather, followed by another, until it seemed that white feathers appeared everywhere I went. It was obviously a sign, and I knew what it was telling me: it was time to start writing my series of books on archangels.

If there's something you intend to do but keep putting off, be aware of white feathers. When the time is right for you to do whatever it is, you'll start seeing white feathers, and you'll continue to see them until you start on whatever it happens to be.

Touch, Sound, and Fragrance

There are many ways in which angels make their presence known. You may feel that someone has touched you—so gently that you're not sure if it actually happened. You may hear beautiful sounds that are so faint you hardly hear them. You may detect the aroma of a gorgeous perfume that isn't familiar to you. These things can happen anywhere. They can occur when you're in a room full of people or sitting at home on your own. Most of the time, you'll wonder if the experience actually happened or if you imagined it. The chances are it's a sign that an angel wants to communicate with you.

It's easy to respond if you're on your own. You can relax in a chair, close your eyes, and silently tell the angel that you're ready to hear what he or she has to tell you. There are two things you can do if you're somewhere with other people. You can close your eyes for a couple of seconds and tell the angel you'll make contact as soon as you're free. If you do this, you'll have to remember to make yourself available as soon as you can. Alternatively, you can excuse yourself and go somewhere where you can be on your own for a short while. A bathroom is a good place for this.

With practice, you'll be able to silently respond, even in the company of others. More than thirty years ago, I was attending an important business meeting with my boss. We were trying to convince the directors of the company to buy a new printing press. It was a major deal, and I wasn't too thrilled when I felt a slight touch on my shoulder. I immediately made silent communication with my guardian angel, as I felt it had to be important if he contacted me in the middle of a sales meeting. My angel told me that the company we were trying to sell the machine to could not afford to buy it, but another company, which he named, would. I silently thanked him and tried to concentrate on the meeting again. When we stood up at the end of the meeting, the company president told us they'd think about our proposal and would come back to us. Of course, they never did, but it didn't matter, as we were able to sell the press to the corporation that my guardian angel mentioned.

Urgent Communication

You're likely to have times in your life when you need help from an angel urgently. I've only ever had to do this once, and it worked miraculously. Many years ago, I was recognized by a group of young born-again Christians who didn't approve of my interests or beliefs. They chased me up the main shopping street in my city, yelling and screaming at me. Just when I thought they were going to catch me, I called out to Michael for help. Instantly, they stopped chasing me, and I was able to go home, shaken but still in one piece.

If you ever find yourself in a similar situation, call on a specific angel immediately. I was so panic-stricken that I simply ran as fast as I could, and it took a while for me to think of asking the angels for help. You might call on your guardian angel, one of the four main archangels, or any other angel who is appropriate for the situation you're in.

You can call in any way you wish, silently or out loud. I can't remember the words I used, but it was something along the lines of "Michael, please help me." A plea of this sort comes directly from the soul and will always be answered.

Don't waste the angel's time by asking for urgent help if you don't need it, but ask as soon as you're in trouble of any sort.

seven

Working with Angels

Now that you've had experience at communicating with angels, we'll go a step further and learn how to work with angels. You need to find somewhere you can work with the angels without being interrupted. Some people are fortunate and have a particular sacred place in their home where they can communicate with angels whenever they wish. Most people have to create a temporary space whenever they want to work with angels. This can be anywhere in your home. Many people use their bedroom, as they can close the door and immediately have the necessary privacy. If you live on your own or have an understanding partner, you can use anywhere you wish. Once you've started using a particular area, it's best to continue using it, as it will develop a special spiritual feel that you'll be able to recognize.

Angel Altar

An altar is a place where you can perform your spiritual practices and communicate with angels. It will become your sacred space. Joseph Campbell had a good description of sacred space: a place where wonder can be revealed. You need to choose this space carefully. In a perfect world, you'd have your altar somewhere in your home where it won't be disturbed. In this scenario, you'd be able to leave it set up all the time. If you live with others and have a permanent altar, you need to make sure that they won't touch or pick up anything that you've placed on your altar.

The altar is where you perform your rituals. You can use any flat surface for this. You might decide to use part of the kitchen or dining room table. You might use the top of a chest of drawers, a desk, or even a shelf. My first altar was a wooden crate with the door from an old cupboard resting on it. It worked perfectly well. At the moment I'm using a coffee table that has a drawer on one side. The drawer is extremely useful, as I can keep spare candles and other items I might need in it.

A friend of mine who travels a great deal in his work, has created a portable altar that he sets up wherever he happens to be. It consists of two candles, a quartz crystal, and an amulet wrapped in a small piece of cloth. He uses the cloth as his altar cloth and arranges the other items on it. He can set up or break down his altar in sixty seconds. In practice, he takes considerably longer than this, as he likes to handle and hold each of the items he uses before placing them into position.

This helps him enter the calm and peaceful state of mind that he needs before performing his spiritual practices.

If you set up your altar outdoors, you might be able to find a suitable flat rock to act as your working surface. If you do this, you'll be participating in an ancient tradition, as the first altars were made from rock or stone. Your outside altar might be in a remote spot well away from civilization, but it could just as easily be in your own backyard.

Your altar needs to be inside your magic circle. You can have it in the middle, if you wish, or place it at the edge of the circle facing east. Of course, if it's in the center of the circle you'll need room to be able to move around it. If you place it at the edge of the circle you can have your altar against a wall that's aligned in the right direction.

You can cover your altar with anything you wish. I have a white tablecloth that works well. Several people I know like to use woven fabric for their altar cloths. A friend of mine bought several linen altar cloths from a liturgical supply company and won't use anything else. Altar cloths can be bought online in a wide variety of patterns and sizes. (You can also buy altars online.)

Once your altar is set up, you can place anything you wish on it. I always use candles and generally have a bowl of flowers on one side. I have a small rock that one of my granddaughters gave to me and usually have a few crystals on display as well. I add other items, such as pen and paper, when they're necessary for the ritual. I also have a jug of water on one side of my altar. This is simply a precautionary measure, as I use candles in my rituals and there's always a possibility of accidentally setting something on fire.

It's important that you find your altar aesthetically pleasing, and you can add anything you wish to make it look more attractive. Everything you place on the altar will gradually gain spiritual energy, and sometimes this is so strong that other people can feel it.

Many people like to energize their sacred space before using it. They might burn incense, ring bells, or beat a drum. Some people use smudge sticks (available at New Age stores) to purify the area before using it. I like to say a prayer before using my altar. As well as energizing your sacred space, this process also enables you to leave your everyday concerns behind and enter into a quiet, meditative state of mind.

Angelic Rituals

A ritual is a series of fixed actions that are performed in a certain order. We all perform a number of personal rituals every day. For instance, when you first wake up in the morning, you probably get out of bed in a certain way and then perform a series of actions that are identical to what you did yesterday and the day before. If you do, you're performing a ritual. Rituals of this sort make life easier, as we're following a regular way of doing certain tasks. Rituals of this sort are done automatically, with little or no conscious thought.

School graduation ceremonies are rituals, as are many religious ceremonies. Weddings, christenings, and funerals are all rituals. There are rituals of courtship that need to be followed. Christians perform the ritual of the Eucharist in which they eat bread and drink wine, because these symbolize the body and blood of Jesus Christ. All religions have their own rituals to help people commune with God. In the past, ritual sacrifices were made to appease the gods. Rituals can also be used to invoke angels.

The first organized ritual I participated in was when I was ten or eleven years old. I was at a Boy Scout camp. One evening, we were sitting around the bonfire after dinner, and our leader asked if we'd like to do something that would dramatically improve our lives. Naturally, we all said yes. He handed around cards and pencils and asked us to write down anything we wanted to change in our lives. He gave us a few examples. If we were impatient, he said, we might write that we didn't like being impatient and wanted to be more patient from now on. If we were jealous, we might write that we didn't like this character trait and wanted to eliminate it from our lives. He told us not to let anyone else see what we'd written. He gave us several minutes to write down whatever we wanted to write. When we'd all finished, he asked us to stand up and walk around the fire seven times while thinking about the changes we wanted to make in our lives. After this, he said a short prayer, and we tossed our pieces of card into the fire. "Look at the smoke," he told us. "It's carrying away all the things that are holding you back. Say goodbye to your old fears and habits."

It took me many years to realize that what I'd participated in was a ritual, but I can still visualize the whole experience as if it happened yesterday. Performing rituals is a good way to make contact with angels.

Ritual When You Need Help

Life isn't easy, and everyone needs help from time to time. You'll find this ritual useful whenever you find yourself needing extra assistance from the angelic kingdom. Your angels are always willing to help you, but you should make every effort to help yourself first. Frequently, you'll find you can resolve a problem without asking for additional help. You should ask the angels for help only if you can't resolve the problem on your own.

1. The best place to perform this ritual is inside your magic circle in front of your altar. If this isn't possible, find somewhere on your own where you can relax and won't be disturbed.

2. Sit down, close your eyes, and take several slow, deep breaths. Allow all the muscles in your body to relax.

3. When you feel completely relaxed, think about your problem or concern.

4. In your mind or out loud, tell your guardian angel or the angel you have chosen for this concern about the problem and what you have done to try to resolve it.

5. Ask for help.

6. Sit quietly for at least sixty seconds and see what comes into your mind. You may feel something, such as a sense of peace or comfort. You may hear a voice or voices as the angels communicate with you. Listen carefully and wait until they've stopped before asking questions.

7. Once you have received all the comfort and information that you need, thank your guardian angel and any other angels that may be involved. Say goodbye and focus on your breathing again for a minute or two.

8. When you feel ready, say thank you one last time, slowly count from one to five, and open your eyes.

Healing Ritual

Angels want you to be fit and healthy and will do all they can to aid your recovery. Angels are also frequently seen when people are dying, and they provide love and support as the soul passes on. Consequently, depending on the person's destiny, the angels help people return to good health and guide the soul to heaven when their life is over. This ritual can be used to heal yourself, friends, loved ones, pets, and humanity as a whole.

You'll need a crystal or some other object that you can imbue with energy. You'll also need a white candle. You can place anything you wish on your altar. You might have a photograph of the person who needs healing or a small object that belongs to him or her. It doesn't matter what you use as long as it's relevant to the ritual. I sometimes have several white candles on the altar while performing this ritual. Depending on how I feel, I'll either stand for the whole ritual or sit down in a chair facing the altar.

1. Prepare your altar and magic circle. If possible, bathe and change into fresh, clean, loose-fitting clothes.

2. Stand outside your circle, holding the white candle with both hands. Take a deep breath, exhale slowly, and enter the circle. Place the candle in the center of your altar and light it. If you're using additional candles, light them, too.

3. Perform the circle of protection (see chapter 6) to surround yourself with the four great archangels.

4. Sit down if you wish. Hold the crystal in your cupped hands. Gaze at the central candle on your altar until

you feel your eyes are becoming tired. Close your eyes and focus on your breathing. As you inhale, visualize yourself filling your body with pure white, healing light. This is the light that you created while doing the circle of protection.

5. Exhale strongly. While doing this, visualize all the built-up negative energy and ill health leaving your body. Replace this negativity with another deep inhalation of white light.

6. Continue doing steps 4 and 5 for as long as you feel necessary.

7. Ask your guardian angel to fill you full of healing energy. If there is a specific part of your body that needs to be healed, visualize your guardian angel sending healing energy directly to the afflicted area.

8. Stay still for a minute or two, visualizing your guardian angel filling you full of healing energy.

9. Visualize the healing energy being absorbed by the crystal. When the time feels right, close your hands around the crystal.

10. Thank your guardian angel for helping you.

11. Allow the pure white light to dissipate and disappear from both your body and the magic circle.

12. Count slowly from one to five and open your eyes. Take a few moments to return to your everyday life. When you feel ready, stretch and get up. Snuff the candle or candles, and carry on with your day. Keep the crystal close to you, possibly in a pocket or purse. Whenever you think of it, hold it in your hands and

visualize the healing energy that the crystal has absorbed flowing out and being transported by your guardian angel to the person, animal, or plant that needs it.

It's a good idea to have something to eat and drink after performing any ritual. This helps to ground you again. You don't necessarily need a meal. I usually have a few nuts and raisins and a glass of water.

If you're performing this ritual for someone else, visualize the person and mentally send the energy to him or her. You can also ask your guardian angel to send your love and healing energy to your friend's guardian angel, confident that it will be passed on.

If you're performing this ritual for all humanity, ask Michael, Raphael, Gabriel, and Uriel to spread your healing energy around the world.

You can ask your guardian angel to send healing energy to your pet and even to garden plants if necessary. Visualize your pet or plant and, in your mind's eye, "see" your guardian angel passing on your love and healing energy.

You can ask whatever angels you wish when doing this exercise. There are a number of healing angels who'll be happy to help you if you ask.

You can ask your angels to help you in other ways to heal others. Whenever my grandmother passed a hospital, she'd pray for the patients inside. I was a child when I saw her doing this, and never thought to ask her what, exactly, she was doing. Consequently, I've no idea if she involved angels in her prayer. I was probably in my thirties when I decided to put my grandmother's idea to the test. Since then I've always sent a prayer to my guardian angel asking him to send healing to the guardian angels of the patients. I also send love and a prayer to the architect of the universe, expressing my gratitude for all the blessings that we all have in our everyday lives.

Whenever someone I know dies, I send a message to my angels asking them to help lead the person's soul to heaven.

Chakras and Chakra Rituals

We are all much more than our physical bodies. There's an almost invisible energy field called the aura that surrounds the bodies of all living things. Ursula Roberts, the famous British psychic, called the aura "a magnetic field of vibration which surrounds every person, in the same way that light surrounds a lighted candle or perfume surrounds a flower" (Roberts 1950, 1). The aura is often shown as a halo around the head and shoulders of saints and angels in religious paintings. The aura extends from two to three feet in all directions from the body. In fact, as it's part of every cell in the body, the aura is actually an extension of the body rather than something that surrounds it.

Inside the aura are a number of energy centers known as chakras. The word *chakra* comes from the Sanskrit word for "wheel." Chakras are usually sensed or felt as revolving, wheel-like discs of energy. They absorb the higher energies, including the universal life force, and transform them into a form that the body can use. They play a vital role in the person's physical, mental, and emotional health. They could be considered to be powerful batteries that energize the entire body. There are many chakras in the human body, but the seven most important ones are in the area of the spine, running from the coccyx to the top of the head.

The Seven Chakras
Root Chakra

Color: Red
Element: Earth
Function: Survival
Glands: Adrenals
Sense: Smell
Desires: Physical contact
Challenge: To think before acting
Keyword: Physical
Angels: Archangels Uriel and Sandalphon

The root chakra is situated at the base of the spine in the area of the coccyx. It keeps us firmly grounded to the earth. It provides a sense of security and self-preservation. It gives energy, vitality, courage, strength, and persistence. This chakra is related to survival and the life force.

The root chakra governs the solid parts of the body, such as the bones, teeth, and nails. An understimulated root chakra creates feelings of fear and nervousness, which often leads to digestion problems.

Sacral Chakra

Color: Orange
Element: Water
Function: Sexuality, pleasure, creativity
Glands: Ovaries, testicles
Sense: Taste

Desires: Respect and acceptance
Challenge: To love and serve others
Keyword: Sociability
Angels: Archangels Gabriel and Chamuel

The sacral chakra is situated in the lower abdomen, approximately two inches below the navel. Because it's related to the water element, it's concerned with the fluidic functions of the body. This chakra provides hope and optimism at an emotional level. Negative emotions, such as anger and resentment, can cause this chakra to be understimulated, causing arthritis; sexual dysfunction; uterus, prostate, kidney, and bladder problems; lower back problems; and loss of personal power.

Solar Plexus Chakra

Color: Yellow
Element: Fire
Function: Will, personal power
Glands: Pancreas
Sense: Sight
Desires: To understand
Challenge: To communicate effectively with loved ones
Keyword: Intellect
Angels: Archangels Jophiel, Uriel, and Michael

The solar plexus chakra is situated between the navel and the sternum. It provides personal power, warmth, confidence, happiness, self-esteem, and a sense of physical well-being. If it's understimulated, it can cause ulcers and liver, pancreas, gall bladder, digestive, and stomach problems.

Heart Chakra

Color: Green
Element: Air
Function: Love
Glands: Thymus
Sense: Touch
Desires: To love and be loved
Challenge: To gain confidence
Keyword: Emotions
Angels: Archangels Raphael and Chamuel

The heart chakra is situated in the center of the chest, near the heart. Not surprisingly, this chakra relates to love, harmony, understanding, and healing. It enhances compassion and respect for yourself and others. If the heart chakra is understimulated, it can cause fear, stress, headaches, and a sense of self-pity. It can also create heart, lung, thymus gland, and immune system problems.

Throat Chakra

Color: Blue
Quadruplicity: Fixed
Function: Communication and creativity
Glands: Thyroid and parathyroid
Sense: Sound
Desires: Inner peace
Challenge: To take risks
Keyword: Concepts
Angel: Archangel Michael

The throat chakra is situated at the level of the throat. It's the chakra of communication and self-expression. At an emotional level, the throat chakra enhances love, idealism, and understanding. If this chakra is understimulated, it can create thyroid, jaw, neck, and shoulder problems.

Brow Chakra

Color: Indigo
Quadruplicity: Mutable
Function: Intuition, thought, and perception
Glands: Pituitary
Desires: To be in harmony with the universe
Challenge: To turn one's dreams into reality
Keyword: Intuition
Angels: Archangels Raziel, Gabriel, and Jophiel

The brow chakra is situated in the forehead, just above the eyebrows. This chakra governs the mind and also makes us aware of our essential spiritual natures. As it's concerned with the spiritual and psychic worlds, it's often referred to as "the third eye." When the brow chakra is understimulated, it creates tension headaches, insomnia, sciatica, asthma, and lung conditions. It can also affect the eyes and the pituitary gland.

Crown Chakra

Color: Violet
Quadruplicity: Cardinal
Function: Union with the divine
Glands: Pineal
Desires: Universal understanding
Challenge: To grow in knowledge and wisdom
Keyword: Spirituality
Angel: Archangel Zadkiel

The crown chakra is situated at the top of the head. Artists often depict it as a halo when painting people who are spiritually evolved. This chakra balances and harmonizes the different sides of our natures. When it is overstimulated, it creates migraine headaches. When it is understimulated, it creates inflammation, heart conditions, eye problems, feelings of uselessness, and depression.

Chakra Healing Ritual

This ritual will enable you to stimulate any chakra that is out of balance. The only essential requirement is a pendulum. You can perform this ritual anywhere, at any time. I like to perform it inside my circle of protection, in front of my altar. I usually have at least one white candle. If possible, I'll have a selection of candles, relating to each of the chakra colors, ready for use if necessary. As usual, have a bath or shower, and change into clean, loose-fitting clothes before performing the ritual.

1. Place the pendulum and a white candle in the center of your altar. Create the circle of protection.
2. Light the candle and gaze at the flame while thinking about your need for healing (or the need of someone else for healing).
3. When you feel ready, pick up your pendulum and ask it to indicate the yes, no, "I don't know," and "I don't want to answer" movements. Do this even if you know the usual responses your pendulum gives you. As the movements can sometimes change, it's a good idea to test the responses every now and again.

4. Ask the pendulum if your root chakra is in balance. If the answer is yes, you can ask the same question about the sacral chakra, and gradually work your way up your spine, as long as the answers remain positive. If the pendulum gives a negative response, ask as many questions as necessary to determine what the problem is.

5. Call on the archangel that works with the particular chakra that is out of balance and ask him to balance the chakra for you. While he's doing this, deliberately move your pendulum in the yes movement. After about sixty seconds, stop moving the pendulum, and ask the archangel if the problem is resolved. The answer will come as a small, still voice in your mind. It may even be a sense that the problem is resolved. If you have any doubts at all about the answer, ask the archangel to reply to you through the pendulum. Hold the pendulum and wait until it gives you a response. You may need to repeat this process a number of times until the chakra is balanced. Thank the archangel who has balanced the chakra for his love and willingness to help.

6. Repeat this process with the next chakra and continue doing this until you've received a positive response to the crown chakra.

7. All of the chakras are now balanced. If you're using colored candles, light the ones that relate to the chakras that were out of balance. Sit and watch them for a few minutes.

8. Take three slow, deep breaths and confirm the success of the ritual by asking your pendulum, "Are all my chakras balanced?"

9. Most of the time, you'll receive a positive response to this question. If you don't, go back to step 4 and repeat the ritual.

10. Once you've received a positive response to your question, relax for a minute or two and then slowly count to five. Get up, snuff out the candles, and leave the circle.

Chakra Color Breathing Ritual

You can also use the seven chakras and their archangels to provide you with a color breathing exercise to enhance your feelings of happiness and well-being. It's a useful ritual whenever you're feeling exhausted and lacking in energy. As always, if possible, have a bath or shower and change into clean, loose-fitting clothes before starting.

1. Create the circle of protection.

2. Sit down comfortably, close your eyes, and take five slow, deep breaths. On each exhalation tell yourself to relax.

3. Once you feel totally relaxed, call on archangel Uriel and ask him to surround you with a pure red energy.

4. Once you feel you're totally surrounded by red, take three slow, deep breaths, inhaling through your nose and exhaling through your mouth. Hold each breath for a second or two before exhaling. Visualize yourself inhaling the red energy with each breath.

5. Repeat steps 3 and 4, calling on archangel Gabriel and pure orange energy.

6. Repeat steps 3 and 4 with Jophiel, Raphael, Michael, Raziel, and Zadkiel, and the colors yellow, green, blue, indigo, and violet, respectively.

7. Complete the exercise by asking all the archangels to fill you with a pure, healing, white light. Relax for as long as you can inside the white light, totally surrounded internally and externally.

8. When you feel ready, take five slow, deep breaths, open your eyes, and get up.

Ritual for Sad and Tragic Events

Whenever we watch the TV news or read a newspaper, we learn about sad and tragic events and happenings around the world. These can range from one-on-one violence all the way up to major wars involving thousands of people. It might be a natural disaster, such as a flood or earthquake. It makes no difference if it involves people you know or is happening to total strangers anywhere in the world. Whatever the bad news happens to be, you can spend a few moments asking your angels to send love, light, and healing to everyone who is caught up in the situation.

You might happen to support a particular side in a disagreement or conflict. Naturally, you're going to want your angels to send loving energy to the people you support. However, you should also send the same love and healing to the people on the other side. You might also send special loving energy to all the innocent people who are simply trying to live their lives but, through no fault of their own, have become caught up in the conflict.

Recently, I read a newspaper report about a murder trial. The mother of the teenage victim stood up in court and said that she forgave the person who'd killed her son. I don't think many people would be able to forgive the perpetrator of a crime that ended the life of a close family member. In addition to forgiving the murderer, she was also giving herself a priceless gift. Rather than holding hate and enmity in her heart, she was freeing herself to get on with her life and give love and attention to the other people she cares for and loves. I have no idea if she used angels while coming to this decision, but one way of doing this would be to ask your angels to send love and light to everyone involved in the tragic situation.

You can ask your angels to send love and light whenever you hear about a tragedy or disaster. Simply close your eyes for a few seconds and ask your angels for help. You can also perform a ritual for a specific situation if you prefer. Here's an example: Let's assume this is a ritual involving two families who live next door to each other and have been arguing about something. It makes no difference to the ritual if the problem is major or trivial.

To prepare, take a bath or shower and put on clean, loose-fitting clothes. Place a white candle in the center of your altar. Create the circle of protection.

1. Light the candle. Sit down in front of it and gaze at it until your eyes feel tired. Close your eyes.
2. Think about the people you love who are involved in the dispute. Visualize them all as clearly as you can.

Remember some of the happy times you've spent with them.

3. Once you've done this, call on your guardian angel and ask him or her to send love and peace to them. Visualize this happening and "see" the expressions on everyone's faces as they become aware of this new energy.

4. Think about the people on the other side of the disagreement. Again, visualize them as clearly as you can. If you experienced some happy moments with them before this problem arose, relive them in your mind. If you can't think of anything, visualize these people enjoying some activity together. See them laughing and enjoying life.

5. Ask your guardian angel to send love and peace to them. Visualize this happening and feel happy as you "see" your neighbors experiencing this loving energy.

6. Visualize a scene in the near future that involves both families, yours and the family you've had the problem with. It might be a shared meal or some other activity. It doesn't matter what it happens to be, as long as you visualize a time when everyone can be happy and at peace with each other again. Enjoy this scene for as long as you can.

7. Ask your guardian angel to fill you with love and light. Thank your guardian angel for all the blessings in your life. Know in your heart that your guardian angel will help you resolve the situation.

8. Allow the white light to gradually disappear.

9. Sit quietly for a while, enjoying the comfort and security that the circle of protection provides. When you feel ready, count from one to five, open your eyes, stretch, and carry on with your day.

I deliberately used a minor event to illustrate this ritual. Let's assume you're wanting to perform a ritual for a major situation, maybe a war in which innocent people are being killed by bombs and air strikes. The first thing that's likely to come to your mind is the appalling situation and all the individual tragedies that are occurring in the war zone every day. In a situation such as this, you need to focus on the positive rather than the negative. In your ritual, ask your angels to send love, light, and healing to everyone involved in the war. This includes the troops on both sides, and the innocent people caught up in the war through no fault of their own. Visualize this healing energy enveloping the entire field of battle and everyone involved. Continue performing this ritual on a regular basis until peace is restored.

I'm frequently asked what to do if the person leading one of the factions is a tyrant who has no concern for individuals and will do anything at all to win. No matter how evil he may be, you'll still need to ask your angels to send love and light to him.

If you're performing a ritual for a natural disaster, ask your angels to send love, light, and healing to everyone caught up in the tragedy. Ask them to guide the souls of everyone who died into the light as quickly and as safely as possible.

Archangel Color Meditation

Everyone has been told at some time that a certain color suits them. This is because everyone has a color that radiates to them. If you receive compliments whenever you wear something in your favorite color, that will probably be the best color for you when doing this meditation.

If no color immediately comes to mind, you can use numerology based on your birth date to determine the correct color to use. You do this by reducing your full date of birth into a number, and then turning that into a color. Here's an example of someone born on July 12, 1973: 7 (month) + 12 (day) + 1973 (year) = 1992. These numbers are then reduced to a single digit: 1 + 9 + 9 + 2 = 21, and 2 + 1 = 3.

There are two exceptions. If your numbers total either 11 or 22 at any stage during the reducing process, you should stop there, rather than reducing them to a single digit. The numbers 11 and 22 are called master numbers in numerology. Here's an example for someone born on November 2, 1996: 11 (month) + 2 (day) + 1996 (year) = 2009, and 2 + 0 + 0 + 9 = 11.

We create a sum from the date of birth because sometimes it's possible to lose the 11s or 22s. If you add up February 29, 1944, in a straight line, you'll end up with number 4: 2 (month) + 2 + 9 (day) + 1 + 9 + 4 + 4 = 31, and 3 + 1 = 4. However, if you create a sum out of this date, you'll find it reduces down to 22.

The number you've created by reducing your date of birth to a single digit (or 11 or 22) is called your life path number in numerology. Each of these numbers relates to a color:

1: Red

2: Orange

3: Yellow

4: Green

5: Blue

6: Indigo

7: Violet

8: Pink

9: Bronze

11: Silver

22: Gold

Now that you've worked out your color, we can move on to the meditation.

1. Do the usual preparations and create the circle of protection.

2. Sit down comfortably, close your eyes, and relax.

3. You have a choice at this stage. You might imagine yourself completely surrounded by your color. Alternatively, visualize yourself walking through a rainbow until you reach your color. Obviously, you can't do that if your color is pink, bronze, silver, or gold.

4. Imagine that you have become this color.

5. Once you can "see" this in your mind, visualize your color growing larger and larger until it completely fills the room you are in. Follow this by visualizing it completely filling the building you're in, followed by

the street, the block, the town, the state, the country, the world, and ultimately the universe.

6. Sense the archangel you want to contact. You'll feel his presence the closer he comes to you.

7. Keep your eyes closed, but visualize the archangel as clearly as you can.

8. When you feel ready, start talking. Tell the archangel what's going on in your life, both positive and negative. Talk about your hopes, dreams, and plans. You'll feel as if you're talking to your best friend and can discuss anything you wish with him or her. Ask as many questions as you wish. You may or may not receive answers immediately. There's no need to feel concerned if you don't receive answers right away. You'll receive them in the next few days, possibly in the form of dreams or sudden thoughts that pop into your mind.

9. When you sense that the conversation is over, thank the archangel. You'll sense the archangel gradually fading away, and you'll be completely surrounded and bathed by your color. Visualize the healing energy of this color washing over the entire universe. Take your time doing this.

10. When you feel ready, thank the universal life force for enabling you to spread love and goodness throughout the universe.

11. Keep your eyes closed long enough for your special color to fade away. Slowly count up to five and open your eyes.

Everyone I know who has performed this meditation has experienced a profound sense of happiness and well-being after this meditation. It's a spiritual, mystical experience that washes away all your concerns and problems and enables you to send healing energy to all mankind as well as to see the world with new eyes.

Crystals and Gemstones

People have admired and treasured gemstones for thousands of years. Crystals are mentioned a number of times in the Bible. The twelve stones on Aaron's breastplate are a good example (Exodus 28:15–21). William Shakespeare mentioned precious stones in many of his plays and sonnets. Throughout the centuries, gemstones have been connected to the angelic realms. Now that you've worked out your color based on your date of birth, you can choose a gemstone that will harmonize with you and help you maintain an even closer connection with your angels.

You can choose a crystal in different ways. You might like to visit a store that sells crystals and allow your intuition to draw you to a stone that is perfect for you. Alternatively, you can do some research first and choose a crystal based on its properties and your particular needs. Finally, you can choose a stone based on its color. Here are some stones that relate to each of the colors:

Red: Coral, ruby, red garnet, rhodonite, and rose quartz
Orange: Carnelian, orange calcite, and sunstone
Yellow: Amber, yellow beryl, citrine, yellow sapphire, and
topaz

Green: Aventurine, chrysoprase, emerald, malachite, and green tourmaline

Blue: Aquamarine, blue lace agate, azurite, lapis lazuli, and sodalite

Indigo: Iolite and indigo sodalite

Violet: Amethyst, purple fluorite, and rhodalite

Pink: Pink tourmaline

Bronze: Bronzite, tiger's eye, and bronze topaz

Silver: Agate, opal, and pearl

Gold: Gold tiger's eye and topaz

Once you've chosen a gemstone, you need to look after it. Don't let anyone else touch it, as you don't want it to be affected by other people's vibrations. Before using your gemstone, you need to cleanse it to get rid of any negativity that it may have picked up before it came into your hands. You can do this in several ways. You might leave it outside overnight and allow the moon's rays to cleanse it. You can bury it in the ground overnight. You can wash it in water, ideally distilled or spring water. You might even use a smudging stick, though in practice I only do this if I'm cleansing a number of gemstones at the same time.

Once your gemstone has been cleansed, you can fill it with angel energy. Hold the crystal in one hand at eye level. Gaze at it for a few seconds, and then tell the gemstone that it's going to be used to bring you even closer to the angelic realms. Ask the gemstone if it's happy to do this. Wait for a response, which will come as a sense of knowing that it's agreed. You might even hear a small voice saying yes. It's more likely to be a feeling of excitement, knowing your gemstone will help you. Thank it, and then hold the gemstone against your brow (third eye) chakra. Invite your guardian angel to activate your gemstone for you. Thank your guardian angel and wrap the gemstone in cotton or silk. Carry the gemstone with you. Whenever you feel the need for angelic contact, hold it loosely in the palm of your hand. If you wish, you can place it in a pocket and fondle it whenever you wish. This will remind you that you're constantly being protected by angelic energy.

eight

Angelic Visitations

Throughout history, people have recorded their experiences with angels. Some of the more famous ones include Joan of Arc, Saint Francis of Assisi, George Washington, Joseph Smith, Charles Lindbergh, and Saint John Bosco.

Joan of Arc

Joan of Arc, the French patriot and martyr, resisted the English during the Hundred Year's War. At the age of thirteen she heard a voice accompanied by a burst of white light. The voice was close and sounded as if someone were talking into her ear. She realized that it was Archangel Michael, who told her she'd be taught by Saint Margaret and Saint Catherine.

Interestingly, Saint Margaret and Saint Catherine were both martyred virgins, and in time, Joan of Arc became one, too. The voices guided and taught her for four years until Archangel Michael gave Joan the task of rescuing France from English domination. Archangel Gabriel also visited her at this time. She was afraid of the voices at first but learned to welcome them. In time she also saw them in visions. Although these were faint, she described Archangel Michael as being a fine-looking gentleman. She became upset whenever anyone asked her to describe the saints and angels she was able to see.

After being rebuffed when trying to speak with a French general, Joan had a vision of the French troops losing a battle against the English in the town of Orléans. When this prediction came true, Joan was able to meet the dauphin. His armies were fighting a losing battle against the British, and he'd reached the stage where he was willing to try anything. Joan persuaded him to let her lead an army that had been formed to relieve Orléans. Riding a white horse and wearing a suit of white armor, Joan and her army defeated the English and forced them to retire. Because of this, she is often referred to as the Maid of Orléans. After this she escorted the dauphin to Reims where he was crowned Charles VII. Shortly afterward, she was captured by the English and tried for heresy and sorcery. At her trial she told the court that she had seen many angels. Joan was found guilty and burned at the stake. Her ashes were tossed into the Seine.

Archangel Michael was considered the protector of France when Joan of Arc was growing up. Consequently, she heard a great deal about him, and it's not surprising that he was the first angel she communicated with.

George Washington

During the winter of 1777, George Washington and his men retreated to Valley Forge after several disastrous encounters with the British army. One day, Washington was working at his desk when an intense light lit up the room. He looked up and saw a beautiful woman wearing a silvery blue dress standing opposite him. He asked her four times what she wanted, but received no answer, except for a slight raising of her eyes. Washington found it impossible to move, and even speech deserted him as he gazed into her eyes. When he told others about the experience later, he said that he didn't think, move, or reason. He did nothing but gaze at the beautiful woman.

The woman finally spoke. "Son of the Republic," she said. "Look and learn!" Washington could now see clouds of vapor in the distance. When this dissipated, he was able to see a huge plain that contained all the countries of the world. The woman repeated the same words again, and Washington was able to see a dark angel floating in the air between America and Europe. This angel dipped his hands into the ocean; and with his right hand she sprinkled water onto America, and with his left onto Europe. Dark clouds formed above both America and Europe and they joined together over the ocean. It then headed to America, which it enveloped in fog. Washington could see flashes of lightning and also hear groans and other sounds from the Americans.

The angel dipped his hands in the ocean again and sprinkled water on both America and Europe. This drew the dark cloud back out to sea where it disappeared from sight. Again the strange woman said, "Son of the Republic, look and learn!" Washington looked at America and saw villages, towns, and cities springing up all across America. The woman spoke again. "Son of the Republic, the end of the century cometh. Look and learn." The angel looked southward, and Washington saw a specter approach America and slowly fly over every settlement in the country. The people came out of their houses and prepared to fight each other. Washington then saw an angel with a crown of light on his forehead. Inside the light was the word "Union." This angel carried the American flag, which he placed between the warring factions, and said, "Remember, ye are brethren." Immediately, the people cast away their weapons and became friends again.

Again the woman said, "Son of the Republic, look and learn!" The dark angel blew three blasts on a trumpet and sprinkled water on Europe, Asia, and Africa. Thick black clouds rose from all three places and joined together in the sky. Washington could see a dark red light in this cloud, which revealed thousands of armed men heading to America by land and sea. The cloud moved to cover all of America, and the armies destroyed all the cities, towns, and villages.

Amongst all the noise created by these battles, George Washington again heard the words, "Son of the Republic, look and learn." The dark angel again raised the trumpet to his lips and blew a single, long blast.

Instantly, an incredibly powerful light shone down on the scene, and the dark cloud dissipated. The angel—who had the crown of light with the word "Union," the national flag in one hand, and a sword in the other—accompanied by thousands of white spirits, descended and joined in the battle to help the American citizens. The strange voice said, "Son of the Republic, look and learn." The dark angel again took water from the ocean and sprinkled it all over America. The remains of the black cloud rolled away, along with the enemy armies, and Washington looked at America, triumphant once again.

Instantly, cities, towns, and villages started appearing, and the angel with the crown of light planted the flag in the center and proclaimed in a loud voice, "While the stars remain, and the heavens send down dew upon the earth, so long shall the Union last." He took off his crown with the word "Union" on it and placed it on the flag. Everyone knelt and said, "Amen."

Washington wrote that the scene started to dissolve and disappear until there was nothing left except for vapor. Once this disappeared, Washington saw the mysterious woman again. "Son of the Republic," she said, "What you have seen is thus interpreted: three great perils will come upon the Republic. The most fearful is the third, but in this greatest conflict the whole world united shall not prevail against her. Let every child of the Republic learn to live for his God, his land and the Union."

George Washington, a devout Christian, believed this vision showed him the birth, progression, and ultimate destiny of the United States.

Saint Francis of Assisi

Saint Francis of Assisi is the only known person to receive a visit from a member of the seraphim, the angels who are closest to God. On September 14, 1224, Francis was fasting and praying in the mountains when he saw a seraph with six shiny, fiery wings descend from heaven. Francis and the seraph had a lengthy conversation, and afterward Francis had the signs of the stigmata on his body. These are the same wounds that Jesus received upon the cross, and Francis was the first person to receive these supernaturally. For the remaining two years of his life, Francis was in constant pain as a result of these wounds.

An old legend says that Saint Francis was one of the very few humans who have been transformed into an angel. He is said to have became the angel Rahmiel. The most notable example of a man who became an angel is the prophet Enoch, who became the great angel Metatron. Jacob became the Archangel Uriel, and the prophet Elijah became Sandalphon. Members of the Church of the Latter-Day Saints believe the angel Moroni was originally a man of the same name.

Saint John Bosco

Saint John Bosco had an extremely unusual guardian angel. It appeared in the form of a huge dog named Grigio. John spent his life looking after homeless boys in Turin, Italy. It was dangerous work, as many of the boys John sought to help robbed him and beat him up. The local citizens weren't happy with what he was doing either, as they wanted the boys to live somewhere else, rather than in their neighborhood.

One night in 1852, John prayed to God and asked for help, as the work was proving too hard for him. Shortly afterward, he noticed a large, gray dog standing behind him. It seemed friendly, but John was nervous because it looked like a wolf. He spoke to the dog, who immediately came up to John and stood beside him. John immediately decided to call the dog Grigio, which is Italian for "gray one." The dog escorted John all the way home and then left.

John didn't see Grigio until he had to walk through a dangerous part of town a few days later. He was nervous until Grigio appeared and again escorted him home. This became a regular routine. Whenever John was in a dangerous area, Grigio appeared. On one occasion, someone fired two shots at John. Grigio chased the gunman, who fled in terror. Grigio saved John on a number of other occasions, too, but his main purpose was to accompany John whenever he had dangerous work to do.

On one occasion, Grigio refused to let John leave his home. Eventually, John gave up, because he knew Grigio had a reason for preventing him from going. Grigio accompanied Saint John Bosco for more than thirty years and even after his death continued to protect the sisters of the Salesian Order that he had founded.

Charles Lindbergh

Charles Lindbergh made the first nonstop, solo flight across the Atlantic Ocean, flying from New York to Paris in his monoplane, the Spirit of St. Louis. In his memoirs he told how he was helped by angels as he made his long and dangerous flight. "These phantoms speak with human voices—friendly, vapor-like shapes, without substance, able to vanish or appear at will, to pass in and out through the walls of the fuselage as though no walls were there" (Lindbergh 1953, 389).

Martin Luther King Jr.

Martin Luther King Jr. had an angelic experience when he was twenty-seven years old. He was a young minister living with his wife, Coretta, and their two-month-old daughter in Montgomery, Alabama. He was opposed to segregation and had agreed to lead the boycott of the Montgomery bus system that had been started by Rosa Park's refusal to give up her seat to a white man. However, King wasn't prepared for the threats and abuse he received for doing this.

Late one night, after receiving a particularly nasty, threatening phone call, he went to the kitchen to heat up some coffee. He started to pray, telling God that he just couldn't face it alone. He suddenly realized there was someone with him. He felt a presence, followed by a voice telling him that he wasn't alone, and he had been chosen to fight against injustice. After this, he knew that no matter what difficulties lay ahead, he would be able to handle them because he had angelic support.

King had been told that if he didn't leave town within three days his home would be bombed. Only days after his experience in his kitchen, someone tossed a bomb into the King's house. Fortunately, no one was hurt, and King felt a sense of peace and resolve. He told the angry crowd who'd gathered outside his house that they should meet hatred with love and should never return violence with violence. His words calmed everyone down and they went home without further incident (Webber 2009).

Ann Cannady

In December 1993, *Time* magazine published a cover story on angels. It included the story of Ann Cannady who was diagnosed with uterine cancer in 1977. Some years earlier, her husband Gary, a retired United States Air Force Master Sergeant, had lost his first wife to the same disease. He wasn't sure that he had enough strength to go through the same ordeal again. Ann and her husband spent eight weeks praying for help.

Someone came to their door three days before Ann was going to hospital for surgery. When Ann opened the door, she saw a large black man with "deep, deep azure blue eyes." She estimated that he was about six foot six inches tall. This man told her that his name was Thomas and her cancer was gone. Ann asked, "How do you know my name, and how do you know I have cancer?" The man replied, "I am Thomas. I am sent by God."

Thomas held up his right palm, and Ann felt an intense heat. Her legs gave way, and she fell to the floor. A strong white light worked its way from her feet to the top of her head. Thomas quoted some words from the Bible: "And with his stripes, we are healed" (Isaiah 55:5).

As soon as Thomas left, Ann called her doctor to tell him she no longer needed surgery. The doctor told her that they'd do a biopsy before the operation, and if it came back positive they'd proceed with the operation. Ann agreed. After the biopsy, her doctor came into her room looking puzzled and confused. He told her the biopsy was completely clean, and that they'd sent the sample to another laboratory for further testing.

Ann returned home free of cancer, and it never returned. This case is well documented. Even Ann's doctor acknowledged that he'd "witnessed a medical miracle" (Gibbs 1993, 59–60).

Today, there seem to be more angelic visitations than ever before. However, this might be because it's easier to tell the world about an angelic experience today than it would have been in the past. If someone living in a small town one hundred years ago had seen an angel, the only people likely to know about it would be family and close friends. Today, that news can be published around the world in a matter of hours.

conclusion

Ever since we were born we've been surrounded by angels. Sadly, most of us ignore them or don't even know they're there. People who live their lives unaware of angels miss out on the amazing sense of joy and comfort that comes from leading a sacred life. Every aspect of your life will be enhanced once you welcome angels into your world. They're there to help you in both the good times and the bad times. Every angelic encounter you have will enhance your faith and increase your contact with the architect of the universe.

It's not always easy to determine which angel you should call upon for a specific situation. Usually, your first choice should be your guardian angel. If you're trying to eliminate negativity from your life, you should call on the angels of the elements. You should also call on them when you need a specific energy. The angels of the earth will ground you. The angels of the air will provide you with energy and the ability to speak your mind. The angels of water will restore your emotional balance, and the angels of fire will provide you with enthusiasm and a desire for knowledge. The angels of the zodiac are a good choice when you're making plans for the future. You can call on the angels of healing at any time, especially when you're stressed or overtired. You should also call on them whenever you, a special person in your life, a family pet, or even a plant needs healing. You can also ask for healing for countries, cities, and people you've never met. You're likely to find it easier to communicate with some angels than with others. This is to be expected, as every angel is different, just as people are. Invest a little time and effort into communicating with the angels who don't respond in the way you expected. They may be testing you, or you may be approaching them the wrong way. In time, you'll have no problems in communicating with any members of the angelic kingdom.

It's now up to you. Create some sacred space for yourself and make yourself available for angelic communication whenever you're inside it. Remain positively expectant and open to angelic communication. You're most likely to receive messages as thoughts, intuitions, or dreams. When you're communicating with angels, you'll experience a sense of the mystical. Albert Einstein, the great physicist and philosopher, wrote,

The most beautiful and most profound emotion we can experience is the sensation of the mystical. It is the sower of all true science. He to whom this emotion is a stranger, who can no longer wonder and stand rapt in awe, is as good as dead. To know what is impenetrable to us really exists, manifesting itself as the highest wisdom and the most radiant beauty which our dull faculties can comprehend only in their most primitive forms—this knowledge, this feeling is at the centre of true religiousness. (Einstein 1931, 6)

I wish you all the best in all your explorations into the angelic world. May you experience the mystical every day of your life.

Angels in Art, Literature, and Music

Angels have played an important role in art and literature for thousands of years. The earliest images of winged figures that may be angels are sculptures made in ancient Egypt approximately six thousand years ago. This predates the book of Exodus in the Bible. Two carved cherubim guarded the Ark of the Covenant in Solomon's temple. The Babylonians destroyed the temple in 586 BCE, and the Ark and the cherubim were destroyed or lost. Angels, or angel-like figures, can be found in classical mythology, Zoroastrianism, Hinduism, Buddhism, and Taoism.

The ancient Greeks and Romans depicted winged figures long before Christianity began. Eros, the Greek god of love, is a good example. He is always depicted as a young man with wings. The goddess Nike, or Victory, was generally shown with wings, encouraging athletes on to victory. The second most popular exhibit in the Louvre in Paris is an eight-foot-tall sculpture of Nike that dates back to about 190 BCE. Nike was a popular goddess in both Greece and Rome.

Angels in Art

The angels we envisage today rely on the art of early Christian artists. Although there are exceptions, Jewish and Islamic artists were generally reluctant to depict angels in their work. This is because of a concern that creating sacred images might encourage people to worship them.

The earliest Christian depictions of angels date back to the third century. However, they were not shown with wings until a century later. Early fifth century mosaics in the nave of the Basilica of Santa Maria Maggiore in Rome show a large number of angels dressed in white togas, with halos and wings (Fletcher 2016).

Usually, Christian artists had two main purposes. Their paintings, frescoes, murals, and sculptures were used to beautify churches. In addition to this, in a time when most people were illiterate, these works of art helped people learn and remember important events from the Bible. Angels were often used to make paintings appear holy and religious and were shown in the background. Other paintings featured angels in depictions of the Eleven Acts of the Holy Angels. These are:

1. *The fall of Lucifer.* This is the story of Lucifer's expulsion from heaven (Revelation 12:3–4). William Blake

and Gustave Doré are two artists who have drawn this incident. A powerful modern statue of Lucifer's fall by the English artist Paul Fryer can be seen in the Holy Trinity Church in Marylebone, London.

2. *Adam and Eve's expulsion from the garden of Eden.* When Adam was expelled from the garden of Eden, God placed cherubims at the east side of the garden of Eden, along with a flaming sword, to guard the way to the Tree of Life (Genesis 3:24). Possibly the most famous depiction of this event was painted by Masaccio in 1425. It can be seen in the church of Santa Maria del Carmine in Florence.

3. *Three angels visit Abraham.* Abraham was visited by three angels who told him that his elderly wife would become pregnant and give birth to a son called Isaac (Genesis 18). The three angels are not identified, but in the Talmud they are said to be Michael, Gabriel, and Raphael (Bava Metzia 86b). The most beautiful example of this theme that I've seen is the painting in the Vatican by Raphael in which three young men (the angels) stand in front of a kneeling Abraham. The young men have no wings, but it's obvious they're angels. This is completely different from Murillo's painting on the same theme, in which the three men seem to be travelers, rather than divine messengers. (This can be seen in the National Gallery of Canada in Ottawa.) Marc Chagall, who was fascinated with angels, painted a modern version of this with winged angels in 1931. It is in the Musée National Message Biblique Marc Chagall in Nice.

4. *The angel of the Lord prevents Abraham from sacrificing his son.* God tempted Abraham by telling him to sacrifice his only son, Isaac. After Abraham had tied up Isaac and placed him on the altar, he took a knife to kill him. An angel of the Lord told him that he had demonstrated his devoutness and should not proceed with the sacrifice (Genesis 22:12). Abraham sacrificed a ram instead of his son. Rembrandt and Caravaggio are two of the many artists who have painted this scene.

5. *Jacob wrestles with an angel.* Jacob spent an entire night wrestling with an angel. When dawn broke and the angel realized he could not defeat Jacob, he touched Jacob's thigh and put it out of joint. The angel blessed Jacob, but refused to tell him his name (Genesis 32:24–30). Rembrandt, Eugène Delacroix, and Paul Gauguin have all produced works of art based on this story.

6. *Angels going up and down Jacob's Ladder.* Jacob had a dream in which he saw a ladder that stretched from earth to heaven. Angels were going up and down this ladder (Genesis 28:12–13). The fresco by the painter Raphael on the ceiling of a room in the Apostolic Palace in Vatican City is probably the most famous example of this theme. Raphael's ladder shows only a few angels. Some depictions show the ladder filled to overflowing with angels.

7. *Shadrach, Meshach, and Abednego are saved from a fiery furnace.* Shadrach, Meshach, and Abednego were three young men who refused to bow down

to King Nebuchadnezzar. Because of this, they were bound and cast into a fiery furnace. The king was astonished when he looked into the furnace and saw four men, unbound and walking in the middle of the furnace. One of them was an angel (Daniel 3:23–28). The English artist J. M. W. Turner's painting of this scene is in the Tate Gallery in London.

8. *An angel slays the entire army of Sennacherib.* When Sennacherib, the Assyrian king, threatened Hezekiah, King of Judah, Hezekiah prayed to God asking for help. The angel of the Lord destroyed all of Sennacherib's forces overnight (II Kings 19:35). Leigh Hunt and Peter Paul Rubens are two artists who have painted this scene.

9. *Raphael protects Tobias.* These paintings tell the story of Tobias's travels. Archangel Raphael advised and protected Tobias on the journey and even told him how to cure his father's blindness (Tobit 5:4). Rembrandt painted many paintings based on this story.

10. *The punishment of Heliodorus.* This story is from the second book of the Maccabees, another book in the Apocrypha. Heliodorus, the chancellor of King Seleucus, was sent to seize money that was intended for the poor from the Temple in Jerusalem. He was beaten by two angels and survived only because Onias, the high priest, prayed for him (II Maccabees 3). In the Apostolic Palace in the Vatican is a famous fresco of this story created by the painter Raphael. Incidentally, on the ceiling of this room is a fresco of Jacob's Ladder, also by Raphael.

11. *The Annunciation.* The Annunciation is the most
famous of the Biblical stories concerning angels.
It tells the story of how Gabriel visited Mary and
told her she would give birth to a son that she was
to name Jesus (Luke 1:26–33). The Annunciation
has been depicted by large numbers of painters and
sculptors since at least the eleventh century, when it
was featured in "Gothic sculpture and stained glass"
(Jameson 1890, 211). A good example of this scene
is "The Annunciation," an engraving by Albrecht
Dürer. Michelangelo's depiction of the Annunciation is one of the only times he drew an angel with
wings. Raphael, Johan van Eyk, Rembrandt, Poussin,
and Tintoretto are just a few of the many artists who
have painted this scene.

Medieval artists were solely concerned with conveying
their spiritual message, and consequently their figures looked
stiff and unlifelike. As time doesn't exist in the angelic kingdom, they were usually depicted as handsome, young men
who never aged. The hierarchies of angels were often represented as circles of heads, with each angel having two, four,
or six wings. It's rare to see more than the two circles of seraphim and cherubim. Artists called these a "glory of angels." A
particularly striking example is the Renaissance painting *The
Coronation of the Virgin* by the Italian artist Ambrogio Ber-
gognone. The angels have bodies draped in robes, and they're
playing musical instruments. As there are said to be angelic
choirs in heaven, it's not surprising that angels are often depicted singing or playing musical instruments.

Giotto was one of the first artists to give his figures personality and to make them appear alive. He was a prolific artist who painted many depictions of angels. His *Flight into Egypt* shows a flying angel protecting Jesus, Mary, and Joseph. Fra Angelico ("Angelic Brother") was a Dominican monk who gained his nickname from his colleagues. He was one of the first artists to paint angels in female form. Leonardo da Vinci painted angels who looked as if they were about to smile. The painter Raphael was named after the great archangel, and as an adult he painted numerous angels. His angels were genderless and sometimes lacked wings. Michelangelo, the Italian Renaissance artist and sculptor, was also named after an angel. His painting on the ceiling of the Sistine Chapel is probably the most famous work of art that includes angels. The angels painted by Correggio looked like beautiful children.

In more recent times, August Rodin, the French sculptor, created lifelike angels. Max Ernst, founder of German Dadaism, painted many angels, as did Paul Klee, the Swiss artist. The most notable artist of recent times to paint angels was Marc Chagall, the Russian artist, who was obsessed with angels. One of his most famous works is *The Fall of an Angel*.

Angels have been so popular in Christian art that it sometimes seems that they're everywhere. On a recent visit to Westminster Abbey in London, I was captivated by the angel frieze in the Henry VII Chapel. The angels are dressed in gowns, and the sashes around their waists are tied with slip knots.

Angels in Literature

Artists have done a great deal to create our perception of what angels look like. Writers have contributed also. John Milton's *Paradise Lost* is a striking example. More than one hundred years ago, the English poet Francis Thompson wrote these opening lines to "Ex Ore Infantium":

> Little Jesus, wast Thou shy
> Once, and just so small as I?
> And what did it feel like to be
> Out of Heaven, and just like me?
> Didst Thou sometimes think of there,
> And ask where all the angels were? (Thompson 1893)

In the *Paradiso* section of his epic poem the Divine Comedy, Dante Alighieri, the Italian poet, used great sensitivity when he wrote about the angels in paradise. When Beatrice, who in the poem is Dante's guardian angel, took him to see heaven, he described the angels like this:

> Their faces all were bright with living flame
> their wings of gold, their other parts so white
> that snow has never reached to that extreme.
> (Paradiso, canto 31, lines 13–15)

William Shakespeare mentioned angels twice in *Hamlet*. The first mention is in act 1, scene 4 when Hamlet says, "Angels and ministers of grace defend us!" (line 39) In the final act, Horatio says goodbye to his dead friend Hamlet: "Goodnight, sweet prince, and flights of angels sing thee to thy rest!" (act 5, scene 2, lines 351–52).

John Milton, wrote the epic poem *Paradise Lost*. Its principal characters are angels. Milton's story explains how humans fell from grace. Satan and the other fallen angels plotted to get Adam to eat the forbidden fruit. Raphael visited Adam and Eve and told them not to go against the will of God. In the course of their conversation, Raphael told Adam about the war in heaven and how Satan and his supporters were sent to hell. Unfortunately, Adam and Eve ate the fruit and Michael escorted them out of paradise. Fortunately, Michael consoled Adam by telling him about the future all the way up to the birth of Christ. Adam was pleased to learn that in the future everyone would have the opportunity to become a Christian.

Naturally, this hugely popular poem included Milton's rather unorthodox ideas about angels. In this poem *Paradise Lost*, angels eat and sometimes bleed. Raphael told Adam that they even enjoy sex:

> Let it suffice thee that thou knows't
> Us happy and without love no happiness …
> Easier than air with air, if spirits embrace,
> Total they mix, union of pure with pure
> Desiring, nor restrained conveyance need
> As flesh to mix with flesh or soul to soul.
> (book 8, 623–628)

In the early nineteenth century, a number of poets wrote epic poems on biblical themes, especially the story of Enoch and his rise to heaven and the downfall of the Watchers, the lustful angels who came down to earth to make love with human beings. *The World Before the Flood* by James Montgomery was published in 1813. It was followed by *The Angel of the World* by George Croly in 1820, *Irad and Adah, a Tale of the Flood* by Thomas Dale in 1821, *The Loves of the Angels* by Thomas Moore in 1822, and *Heaven and Earth* by Lord Byron in 1823. These poems are seldom read today but were very popular in their time.

Incidentally, Lord Byron also wrote humorously about angels, as this example from *The Vision of Judgment* by Quevedo Redivivus (pseudonym) shows:

> The angels all were singing out of tune,
> And hoarse from having little else to do,
> Excepting to wind up the sun and moon
> Or curb a runaway young star or two. (Byron 1828, 487)

Leigh Hunt's poem *Abou Ben Adhem*, about racial and religious tolerance, has become one of the most popular angel poems of all. It starts,

> Abou Ben Adhem (may his tribe increase!)
> Awoke one night from a deep dream of peace,
> And saw, within the moonlight in his room,
> Making it rich, and like a lily in bloom,
> An angel writing in a book of gold.
> (quoted in *By Heart* 1965, lines 1–5)

Emily Dickinson, the American poet, wrote a great deal about angels. I particularly like *Angels in the Early Morning,* which describes smiling, flower-picking angels.

Another famous poem about angels is *Sandalphon* by Henry Wadsworth Longfellow. Here is the first verse:

> Have you read in the Talmud of old,
> In the Legends the Rabbins have told
> Of the limitless realms of the air,
> Have you read it,—the marvellous story

Of Sandalphon, the Angel of Glory,
  Sandalphon, the Angel of Prayer? (Longfellow 1858)

Novelists also wrote about heaven and angels. Mark Twain, the great American writer, wrote a book called *Captain Storm-field's Visit to Heaven*. This tells the story of a crusty sea captain who dies and goes to heaven. Once there he demands his halo and harp. Using his famous sense of humor, Mark Twain gently mocks the traditional view of angels.

Mark Twain also wrote a short story called "A Singular Episode: The Reception of Sam Jones in Heaven." In this story the Archbishop of Canterbury discovers that angels speak Chinese with "a heavenly accent." Sam Jones steals the archbishop's train pass and replaces it with his own. This means they get misidentified in heaven, and Sam preaches to everyone in heaven using "language that made the place fairly shudder." In less than a week, everyone had left heaven, leaving Sam Jones there on his own.

George Bernard Shaw, the English dramatist, had a good sense of humor, too. He wrote a short story called *Aerial Football: The New Game*, which tells the story of the souls of a haughty English bishop and his charwoman. He arrived in heaven expecting to be treated with the same reverence and respect he'd enjoyed on earth. When he found he was treated in exactly the same way as everyone else, he walked out. However, he soon returned. He took off his miter, stuffed his bishop's apron inside, and with a big yell kicked it high in the air. All the angels and saints yelled too, and soon they were playing a game of aerial football (soccer) using his miter as a ball.

Most stories about angels are not humorous. *A Very Old Man With Enormous Wings*, a short story by the Columbian author Gabriel García Márquez, tells about an old, confused angel who is found by a couple in their courtyard. They realize he's an angel and keep him in their chicken coop for several years. People come to visit him and even steal feathers from his wings, hoping for a miracle. Finally, the couple start charging people money to see the angel. A traveling freak show arrives in the village, and the inhabitants lose interest in the angel as they flock to see a spider woman and other attractions. The angel finally starts regaining his strength. His feathers grow back, and he spends the evenings singing sea shanties. One day, he stretches his wings and flies back to heaven. The moral of the story is that humans fail to appreciate the incredible wonders that surround us.

Bernard Malamud wrote a short story called *The Angel Levine* about a Jewish tailor in New York and his black guardian angel. Initially, the tailor refuses to believe that his guardian angel is actually an angel at all. It's only when his problems continue to mount that he finally lets his guardian angel help him. This story was made into a film starring Zero Mostel and Harry Belafonte in 1970.

This Present Darkness by Frank Peretti, a well-known and prolific Christian writer, was published in 1986. It tells the story of angels who overpower demons in a small college town. This book remained on the Christian Booksellers Association top ten best sellers list for more than 150 weeks and has sold more than two million copies. A sequel, *Piercing the Darkness*, appeared in 1989.

The Vintner's Luck by New Zealand author Elizabeth Knox became a worldwide success in 1998. It tells the story of Xas, a gay angel, and his love affair with Sobran Jodeau, a poor French winemaker, in the early nineteenth century. They meet when Xas catches Jodreau, who is about to fall into a drunken stupor. Jodeau becomes convinced that Xas is his guardian angel, and the two meet once a year for decades. The book is largely a story about the love Jodeau has for his wife, his mistress, and his angel. *The Vintner's Luck* was made into a film (*A Heavenly Vintage*) in 1989.

Stories about angels have become increasingly popular over the last twenty years. Many of these challenge traditional beliefs about angels and include romances and adventure stories with angels playing important roles. Examples include the *Kissed by an Angel* trilogy by Elizabeth Chandler, and *Angelology* and *Angelopolis*, both by Danielle Trussoni. A more humorous approach is Sharon Creech's children's novel, *The Unfinished Angel*. This tells the story of an angel who is clearly missing some of the usual attributes of angels, including the ability to speak English without using malapropisms and made-up words.

Angels in Movies

Angels have appeared in many movies over the years. Arguably, the best of these is the ever-popular *It's a Wonderful Life*, which was released in 1946. The only American movie about angels that preceded it was the Oscar-winning *Here Comes Mr. Jordan,* which was released in 1941. This tells the story of a young boxer named Joe who crashes his plane while on his way to a fight. His guardian angel transports him to heaven. As he died fifty years earlier than he should have, he's given a new life as a fun-loving millionaire.

Frank Capra's amazing movie *It's a Wonderful Life*, starring Jimmy Stewart, is still popular even though it came out way back in 1946. George Bailey, who has devoted his life to helping the citizens of his small town, is about to commit suicide as he thinks he'll be blamed for the loss of eight thousand dollars from his small business. His guardian angel, Clarence, who has come to earth to earn his wings, helps the depressed man by showing him what the world would be like if he'd never existed.

Angels in the Outfield (1951) is another popular angel movie. It proved so popular it was remade in 1994. This movie tells how a group of angels reverse the bad season a major league baseball team is having and win the pennant. This angelic interest in baseball is caused because a young boy asks his father when they'd become a family again. He replies, "When the Angels win the pennant." He takes his father's words literally, and prays to God, asking him to help the Angels win. (In the 1951 original version, it was a young orphan girl who saw angels.)

Michael (1996) stars John Travolta as the Archangel Michael who is living with an elderly woman in a remote part of Iowa. Two journalists are sent to investigate and find that Michael does, in fact, have wings, but also possesses an active libido and a penchant for beer and rather colorful language.

Gabriel (2007) is set in purgatory. Gabriel assumes a human form to try to return light to a place that has become dark and dangerous. Six archangels have already tried to do this without success. Gabriel has to defeat Sammael, a fallen angel, to enable good to overcome evil.

Legion (2010) is the story of a legion of angels who have been sent by God to bring on the apocalypse. Archangel Michael is unhappy with this decision, and with a group of strangers he meets in a diner, tries to save the world.

There are many movies featuring bad angels, and a number that involve angels who want to become humans, usually because they've fallen in love with a human. A good example is the German movie *Wings of Desire* (1987) that tells the story of an angel who falls in love with a human and wants to become human himself. There is no guarantee that he'll ever meet the object of his love once he becomes human, either. *Wings of Desire* was remade in English as *City of Angels* in 1998. *I Married an Angel* (1942), *Date with an Angel* (1987), *Always* (1989), and *Faraway, So Close!* (1993) are just some of the movies about a romantic attraction between an angel and a human.

Angels in Television

Angels are popular in television shows, too. Michael Landon, who had previously starred in *Bonanza* and *Little House on the Prairie*, played the role of an angel named Jonathan Smith in the successful series *Highway to Heaven*, which ran from 1984 to 1989.

The hugely popular drama series *Touched by an Angel* ran from 1994 to 2003. The main characters are three angels who are sent to Earth to remind people that God hasn't forgotten them and still loves them.

Dominion, a postapocalyptic drama, ran for two seasons from 2014 to 2015. This series has two archangels, Gabriel and Michael, fighting against each other after God disappears.

Angels in America (2003) is an HBO miniseries about six New Yorkers whose lives intersect in different ways. One of the characters is a gay man suffering from AIDS who is visited by an angel who has ulterior motives.

Fallen (2006) is a miniseries about a teenage boy who discovers he is a Nephilim (one parent human, the other an angel), and tries to lead a normal life despite having to evade warrior angels who are dedicated to wiping out all the Nephilim.

Angels in Classical Music

Composers have tried to illustrate the sound of angels' singing since at least the time of the sixteenth-century composer Giovanni Palestrina. His *Missa Papae Marcelli* mass is thought to have been composed after he heard angel voices singing the opening bars to him. In the "Sanctus" in his Mass in B Minor, Johann Sebastian Bach used ascending scales, repeated motifs, and harmony to illustrate the different ranks of angels. *The Messiah* by George Frideric Handel has several references to angels, including "Glory to God." Richard Wagner wrote *Der Engel* ("The Angel"), which is a song about a guardian angel. The last movement of Gustav Holst's Symphony no. 8 in E-flat Major ("Symphony of a Thousand") includes an angelic chorus. In one of his less successful operas, *Giovanna d'Arco* (Joan of Arc), Giuseppe Verdi contrasts good and bad angels by the type of music they sing. The good angels sing church music, and the bad angels sing a song suitable for a bordello. Gustav Mahler's Fourth Symphony has a soprano as an angel celebrating divine joy. Incidentally, he also used angel motifs in his second and third symphonies. Sergei Prokofiev wrote *The Fiery Angel*, an opera that wasn't performed until after his death. Rather than waste the music, he made use of some of it in his Third Symphony. Part of this music involves an angel who brings music to a young girl.

Angels in Christmas Hymns and Carols

Not surprisingly, angels appear frequently in music that celebrates Christmas. Possibly the first carol to mention angels is The Angel's Song by Orlando Gibbons. Since then, many Christian Christmas songs have mentioned angels. These include "Angels from the Realms of Glory," "Angels We Have Heard On High," "Go Tell It on the Mountain," "God Rest Ye Merry Gentlemen," "Hark! The Herald Angels Sing," "It Came upon a Midnight Clear," "I Saw Three Ships," "I Wonder as I Wander," "Mary's Boy Child," "O Come All Ye Faithful," "O Holy Night," "O Little Town of Bethlehem," "Once in Royal David's City," "Silent Night," "The First Noel," "What Child Is This?," and "While Shepherds Watch Their Flocks."

Angels in Popular Music

Angels are mentioned regularly in popular music. The doowop song "Earth Angel" became a hit for the Penguins in 1954. "My Special Angel" became a hit for Bobby Helms in 1957. In 1960 Rosie and the Originals released "Angel Baby." It became a huge hit for fifteen-year-old Rosie Hamlin and stayed in the charts for twelve weeks. John Lennon recorded his version of the song in 1973. The sad ballad "Teen Angel" reached the top position on US *Billboard* Hot 100 in February 1960. "Pretty Little Angel Eyes" was recorded by Curtis Lee in 1961. "Johnny Angel" was Shelley Fabares debut song in 1962. She was Donna Reed's daughter in *The Donna Reed Show* and sang it first on the show. Elvis Presley released "(You're the) Devil in Disguise" in 1963. It included the line "You walk like an angel." "Angel of the Morning" became a worldwide hit in 1968 and has been recorded by many artists over the years. "Seven Spanish Angels" was recorded by Ray Charles and Willie Nelson in 1984. ABBA released "I Have a Dream" in late 1979. It included a verse that started with the line "I believe in angels." Madonna wrote and recorded "Angel" in 1985. One of the most popular songs in Andrew Lloyd Webber's *The Phantom of the Opera* (1986) is "Angel of Music." Bette Midler had an international hit in 1988 with a song that could almost be called an angel song, "Wind Beneath My Wings." The Jeff Healey Band's recording of "Angel Eyes" was the seventeenth most popular single in the US in 1989. "How Do You Talk to an Angel," with Jamie Walters as the lead singer, became the number one hit on the US *Billboard* Hot 100 in November 1992. It was the theme for the TV series *The Heights,* which aired from August to November 1992. In 1997, "Angel of Mine" was recorded by the British girl group Eternal. The American version, released by Monica in 1998, reached number one and became the sixty-second most popular single in the US 1990s chart. Robbie William's biggest hit, "Angel," which he cowrote with Guy Chambers, became his biggest-selling single in 1997. Apparently, they wrote this song in less than twenty-five minutes.

Many country music songs make references to angels. These include "I Can See an Angel" by Patsy Cline, "Angels Watching Over Me" by the Oak Ridge Boys, "Angel Flying Too Close to the Ground" by Willie Nelson, "Angels" by Randy Travis, and "And the Angels Cried" by Alan Jackson and Alison Krauss.

Angels for Different Purposes

Over the years, thousands of angels have been named. Many of them have a strong interest in certain subjects and can be called upon whenever you need help in a particular area. Here is a list of different purposes and the angels that are associated with them:

Addictions (breaking): Baglis, Raphael, Uriel

Adversity: Caliel, Sitael

Anger (controlling): Affafniel, Hemah, Qispiel

Animals (protecting and healing): Afriel, Behemiel, Hariel, Jehiel, Nemamiah

Arts (success in): Akriel, Haamiah, Hariel

Birds (protection of): Anpiel

Blessings (to send): Hael

Business (success in): Anauel, Ieiaiel, Mihr

Childbirth: Amariel, Armisael, Gabriel, Rachmiel, Temeluch, Zuriel

Children: Nemamiah

Communication: Iezalel

Compassion: Hanael, Rahmiel, Raphael, Sophia, Tiphareth

Conception: Armisael, Lailah

Confidence: Ihiazel, Vehujah

Contemplation: Cassiel

Courage: Chamuel, Malahidael, Metatron, Michael, Raphael, Samael

Creativity: Anael, Asariel, Jophiel, Liwel, Teiazel, Vehael

Divination: Adad, Isaiel, Paschar, Teiaiel

Divorce: Bethnael, Gabriel, Michael, Pallas, Raphael, Uriel

Dreams (to encourage): Gabriel

Emotions (controlling): Muriel

Employment: Anauel, Uriel

Evil (to ward off): Ambriel

Evil Eye (preventing): Rahmiel, Sariel

Faith (to encourage): Abadiel, Raguel, Uzziel

Family: Jeliel, Verchiel

Fertility: Abariel, Akriel, Anahita, Armisael, Borachiel, Gabriel, Samandriel

Forgetfulness: Ansiel, Pathiel

Forgiveness: Balthial, Chamuel, Uzziel

Friendship: Amnediel, Anael, Cambiel, Charmeine, Mebahel

Gardening: Ariel, Uriel

Good Fortune: Barchiel, Poiel

Guidance: Sariel

Happiness: Eiael, Lauviah, Nilaihah

Harmony (between people): Cassiel, Gavreel, Haziel

Hatred (to eliminate): Gabriel

Healing: Ariel, Gabriel, Michael, Raphael, Sariel, Uriel

Health (good): Lelahel

Home: Cahatel, Iezalel, Uriel

Impulsiveness: Caliel

Independence: Adnachiel

Injury (mental and physical): Alimon

Inner peace: Gavreel

Intellect: Asaliah, Zachariel

Jealousy (to release): Ariel, Gabriel, Uriel

Justice: Soterasiel

Knowledge: Asaliah, Raphael, Raziel, Uriel

Liberty: Terathel

Lost Items: Rochel

Love: Adriel, Amnediel, Anael, Ardifiel, Asmodel, Charmeine, Donquel, Gabriel, Hagiel, Nilaihah, Rachiel, Rahmiel, Raphael, Theliel, Uzziel

Lucidity: Hakamiah

Marriage (harmonious): Amnixiel, Gabriel

Meditation: Iahhel

Memory: Zadkiel

Money: Anauel, Zadkiel

Morality: Pahaliah

Music: Israfil, Sandalphon

Obedience: Mitzrael

Passion (to invoke): Miniel

Patience: Achaiah, Gabriel

Peace: Cassiel, Gabriel, Gavreel, Melchizedek, Valoel

Persistence: Samael

Philosophy: Mebahiah

Prayer: Gabriel, guardian angel, Michael, Raphael, Salaphiel

Pregnancy (protection during): Avartiel, Badpatiel, Lailah

Problem Solving: Achaiah

Property: Adriel

Prosperity: Anauel, Ariel, Barbelo, Sachiel, Uriel

Protection: Ambriel, archangels, guardian angel, Melahel

Psychic Skills (to develop): Amael, Azrael, Colopatiron, Paschar, Remiel

Punishment (suitable): Hutriel

Purification: Tahariel

Repentance: Michael, Penuel, Raphael, Shepherd

Science: Hariel, Raphael

Sensitivity: Umabel

Serenity: Cassiel

Sleep (to encourage): Gabriel, Rapahel

Solutions (to problems): Jeliel

Spirituality: Elemiah, Haamiah, Jegudiel, Micah

Stress: Raphael

Study: Akriel, Asaliah, Harahel, Iahhel, Metatron, Michael, Pallas, Raphael, Uriel, Vesta, Zachariel

Success: Gazriel, Malkiel, Perpetiel

Tears: Sandalphon

Travel: Elemiah

Trust: Tezalel

Truth: Amitiel

Wisdom: Damabiah, Sagnessagiel

references

Adler, Mortimer J. 1982. *The Angels and Us*. New York: Macmillan.

Anselm. 2008. *Anselm of Canterbury: The Major Works*. Edited by Brian Davies and G. R. Evans. Oxford: Oxford University Press.

The Ante-Nicene Fathers: The Twelve Patriarchs, Excerpts and Epistles, The Clementina, Apocrypha, Decretals, Memoirs of Edessa and Syriac Documents, Remains of the First Ages. 1886. Edited by Alexander Roberts, James Donaldson, Arthur Cleveland Coxe, and Allan Menzies. New York: Charles Scribner's Sons.

Alighieri, Dante. 1962. *The Divine Comedy, Part 3: Paradise.* Translated by Dorothy L. Sayers and Barbara Reynolds. London: Penguin Books Limited.

———. 2007. *Dante: Paradiso.* Translated and edited by Robin Kirkpatrick. London: Penguin Books.

Aquinas, Thomas. 1974. *Summa Theologica.* Translated by the Fathers of the English Dominican Province. Reprinted, Internet Sacred Text Archive. Accessed July 14, 2016. http://www.sacred-texts.com/chr/aquinas/summa/index.htm.

Baqli, Ruzbihan. 1997. *The Unveiling of Secrets: Diary of a Sufi Master.* Translated by Carl W. Ernst. Chapel Hill: Parvardigar Press.

Barrett, Francis. (1801) 1989. *The Magus.* Reprint, Wellingborough, UK: Aquarian Press.

Barth, Karl. 1960. *Church Dogmatics,* vol. 3, part 3. Translated by G. W. Bromiley and R. J. Ehrlich. Edinburgh: T & T Clark.

Bell, James Stuart, ed. 2012. *Angels, Miracles, and Heavenly Encounters: Real-Life Stories of Supernatural Events.* Minneapolis: Bethany House Publishers.

Biriotti, Sophie, ed. 1997. *The Possibility of Angels: A Literary Anthology.* San Francisco: Chronicle Books.

Black, Matthew. 1985. *The Book of Enoch or 1 Enoch.* Leiden, Netherlands: E. J. Brill.

Bloom, Harold. 1996. *Omens of Millennium: The Gnosis of Angels, Dreams, and Resurrection.* New York: Riverhead Books.

Burnham, Sophy. 1990. *A Book of Angels*. New York: Ballantine Books.

Bussagli, Marco. 2007. *Angels*. New York: Abrams Books.

By Heart: An Anthology of Memorable Poems Chosen from All Periods. 1965. Edited by Francis Maynell. London: Nonesuch Press.

Byron, George Gordon. 1828. *The Works of Lord Byron: Including the Suppressed Poems*. Paris: A. and W. Galignani. HathiTrust. https://babel.hathitrust.org/cgi/pt?id=hvd.hwnsbp;view=1up;seq=11.

Charles, R. H., ed. 1908. *The Greek Versions of the Testaments of the Twelve Patriarchs*. Oxford: Clarendon Press.

———, trans. and ed. 1912. *The Book of Enoch or 1 Enoch*. Oxford: Oxford University Press.

———, ed. 1913. *The Apocrypha and Pseudepigrapha of the Old Testament in English*. Oxford: Clarendon Press.

Chase, Steven, trans. and ed. *Angelic Spirituality: Medieval Perspectives on the Ways of the Angels*. New York: Paulist Press, 2002.

Conybeare, Frederick G., trans. 1898. "The Testament of Solomon." Article in *Jewish Quarterly Review* 11 (October): 15–45. Edited by Joseph H. Peterson for Esoteric Archives, 1997. http://www.esotericarchives.com/solomon/testamen.htm.

Cortens, Theolyn. 2003. *Living with Angels: Bringing Angels into Your Everyday Life*. London: Piatkus.

———. 2005. *Working with Your Guardian Angel: An Inspirational 12-Week Programme for Finding Your Life's Purpose.* London: Piatkus.

Cruz, Joan Carroll. 2009. *Angels & Devils.* Rockford, IL: TAN Books.

Davidson, Gustav. 1967. *A Dictionary of Angels: Including the Fallen Angels.* New York: The Free Press.

DeStefano, Anthony. 2012. *Angels all Around Us: A Sightseeing Guide to the Invisible World.* Colorado Springs: Image Books.

Dickason, C. Fred. (1995) 1975. *Angels Elect and Evil.* Chicago: Moody Press. Rev. ed.

Einstein, Albert. 1937. *Living Philosophies.* New York: Simon and Schuster.

Evans, Hilary. 1987. *Gods, Spirits, Cosmic Guardians: A Comparative Study of the Encounter Experience.* Wellingborough, UK: The Aquarian Press.

Field, M. J. 1971. *Angels and Ministers of Grace: An Ethnopsychiatrist's Contribution to Biblical Criticism.* London: Longman Group Limited.

Fletcher, Adrian. 2016. "The Major Basilica of Santa Maria Maggiore: Triumphal Arch Mosaics (c430)." Paradox Place. Accessed July 16. http://www.paradoxplace.com/Perspectives/Rome%20&%20Central%20Italy/Rome/Rome_Churches/Santa_Maria_Maggiore/Santa_Maria_Maggiore_Triumphal_Arch/Santa_Maria_Maggiore_Mosaics_T.htm.

Fodor, Nandor. 1933. *Encyclopaedia of Psychic Science.* London: Arthurs Press.

Garfield, Laeh Maggie, and Jack Grant. 1995. *Angels and Companions in Spirit*. Berkeley, CA: Celestial Arts Publishing.

Garrett, Duane A. 1995. *Angels and the New Spirituality*. Nashville, TN: Broadman & Holman Publishers.

Garrett, Greg. 2015. *Entertaining Judgment: The Afterlife in Popular Imagination*. New York: Oxford University Press.

Georgian, Linda. 1994. *Your Guardian Angels: Use the Power of Angelic Messengers to Empower and Enrich Your Life*. New York: Simon and Schuster.

Gibbs, Nancy. 1993. "Angels Among Us." *Time,* December 27, 59–60.

Ginzberg, Louis. (1909–38) 2003. *Legends of the Jews.* 2 vols. Philadelphia, PA: The Jewish Publication Society.

González-Wippler, Migene. 1999. *Return of the Angels*. St. Paul, MN: Llewellyn Publications.

Goddard, David. 1996. *The Sacred Magic of the Angels*. York Beach, ME: Samuel Weiser.

Graham, Billy. (1975) 1986. *Angels: God's Secret Agents*. Rev. ed. Dallas, TX: Word Publishing.

Guiley, Rosemary Ellen. 1994. *Angels of Mercy*. New York: Pocket Books.

———. 1996. *Encyclopedia of Angels*. New York: Facts on File.

Hanegraaff, Wouter J. 1997. *New Age Religion and Western Culture: Esotericism in the Mirror of Secular Thought*. Albany, NY: SUNY Press.

Harkness, Deborah E. 1999. *John Dee's Conversations with Angels.* Cambridge: Cambridge University Press.

Hildegard of Bingen. 1985. *Scivius* III. *Hildegard con Bingen's Mystical Visions.* Translated by Bruce Hozeski. Santa Fe, NM: Inner Traditions.

Hodson, Geoffrey 1932. *The Coming of the Angels.* London: Rider and Company.

———. 1952. *The Kingdom of the Gods.* Adyar, India: The Theosophical Publishing House.

Hoffman, Joel M. 2014. *The Bible's Cutting Room Floor: The Holy Scriptures Missing From Your Bible.* New York: Thomas Dunne Books.

Holy Bible in the King James Version. 1984. Nashville, TN: Thomas Nelson Publishers.

Humann, Harvey. 1986. *The Many Faces of Angels.* Marina del Rey, CA: DeVorss & Company.

Jameson, Anna. (1852) 1890. *Legends of the Madonna.* London: Longmans, Green and Company.

———. (1857) 1895. *Sacred and Legendary Art.* Vol. 1. Boston: Houghton Mifflin and Company, 1895. First published 1857.

Jeremiah, David. 1996. *What the Bible Says about Angels.* Sisters, OR: Multnomah Publishers, Inc.

Jerome. 2008. *The Fathers of the Church*, vol. 117: *Commentary on Matthew.* Translated by Thomas P. Scheck. Washington, DC: The Catholic University of America Press.

Joel. 1836. *Ioelis chronographia compendaria.* Edited by Immanuel Bekker. Bonn: Impensis Ed. Weberi.

John of Damascus. (1899) 2009. *An Exposition of the Orthodox Faith*. Book II. In *Nicene and Post-Nicene Fathers*, second series, vol. 9. Translated by E.W. Watson and L. Pullan and edited by Philip Schaff and Henry Wace. Buffalo, NY: Christian Literature Publishing Co. Revised and edited by Kevin Knight. New Advent. http://www.newadvent.org/fathers/33042.htm.

John Paul II. 1997. "Regina Caeli." Easter Monday address. March 31. Libreria Editrice Vaticana. http://w2.vatican.va/content/john-paul-ii/en/angelus/1997/documents/hf_jp-ii_reg_19970331.html.

Jovanovic, Pierre. 1995. *An Inquiry into the Existence of Guardian Angels: A Journalist's Investigative Report*. New York: M. Evans and Company, Inc.

Kabbani, Shaykh Muhammad Hisham. 1995. *Angels Unveiled: A Sufi Perspective*. With a preface by Sachiko Murata. Chicago: KAZI Publications.

Keck, David. 1998. *Angels and Angelology in the Middle Ages*. Oxford: Oxford University Press.

Lambert, Gray. 2013. *The Leaders Are Coming!: Whom Will You Follow?* Bloomington, IN: Westbow Press.

Lindbergh, Charles A. 1953. *The Spirit of St. Louis*. New York: Charles Scribner's Sons.

Longfellow, William Wadsworth. 1858. *The Courtship of Miles Standish and Other Poems*. Boston: Ticnor and Fields.

Loxton, Howard. 1995. *The Art of Angels*. London: Regency House.

Meyer, Marvin. 2005. *The Secret Gospels of Jesus*. London: Darton, Longman and Todd Limited.

Miller-Russo, Linda, and Peter Miller-Russo. 1999. *Angelic Enlightenment: A Personal Process*. St. Paul, MN: Llewellyn Publications.

Milton, John. (1909–14) 2001. *Harvard Classics,* Vol 4: *The Complete Poems of John Milton.* Edited by Charles W. Eliot. New York: P.F. Collier & Son. Bartleby.com, 2001. http://www.bartleby.com/4/.

Moolenburgh, H. C. 1984. *A Handbook of Angels*. Saffron Walden, UK: The C. W. Daniel Company Limited.

Nahmad, Claire. 2004. *Summoning Angels: How to Call on Angels in Every Life Situation*. London: Watkins Publishing.

Newhouse, Flower A. 1950. *Rediscovering the Angels*. Escondido, CA: The Christward Ministry.

———. 1955. *The Kingdom of the Shining Ones*. Escondido, CA: The Christward Ministry.

———. 1995. *Angels of Nature*. Edited by Stephen Isaac. Wheaton, IL: Quest Books.

Nichols, Sallie. 1980. *Jung and Tarot: An Archetypal Story.* New York: Weiser Books.

Oppenheim, A. Leo. 1964. *Ancient Mesopotamia: Portrait of a Dead Civilization*. Chicago: University of Chicago Press.

Oxford Univeristy and Cambridge University. *The Apocrypha: translated out of the Greek and Latin tongues: being the version set forth A.D. 1611 compared with the most ancient authorities and revised A.D. 1894.* 1895. Oxford:

Oxford University Press; Cambridge: Cambridge University Press.

Parente, Alessio. 1983. *"Send Me Your Guardian Angel" Padre Pio*. Amsterdam, NY: The Noteworthy Company.

Parisen, Maria, comp. 1990. *Angels & Mortals: Their Co-Creative Power*. Wheaton: Theosophical Publishing House.

Poloma, Margaret, and George Gallup. 1990. *Varieties of Prayer*. Harrisburg, PA: Trinity Press International.

Pseudo-Dionysius. 1987. *Pseudo-Dionysius: The Complete Works*. Translated by Colm Luiheid. Mahwah, NJ: Paulist Press.

Redfield, James, Michael Murphy, and Sylvia Timbers. 2002. *God and the Evolving Universe*. New York: Jeremy P. Tarcher/Putnam.

Richards, Larry. 1998. *Every Good and Evil Angel in the Bible*. Nashville, TN: Thomas Nelson Inc.

Roberts, Ursula. 1950. *The Mystery of the Human Aura*. London: The Spiritualist Association of Great Britain.

Roland, Paul. 1999. *Angels: An Introduction to Angelic Guidance, Inspiration and Love*. London: Piatkus.

Ronner, John. 1993. *Know Your Angels: The Angel Almanac with Biographies of 100 Prominent Angels in Legend and Folklore, and Much More*. Murfreesboro, TN: Mamre Press.

Ronner, John, and Fran Gangloff. 2000. *The Angel Calendar Book: 365 Days Tied to the Angels*. Murfreesboro, TN: Mamre Press, 2000.

Russell, Jeffrey Burton. 1998. *A History of Heaven: The Singing Silence.* Princeton University Press.

Sardello, Robert, ed. 1994. *The Angels.* Dallas, TX: Dallas Insitute Publications.

Schneider, Petra, and Gerhard K. Pieroth. 2000. *Archangels and Earthangels: An Inspiring Handbook on Spiritual Helpers in the Metaphysical and Earthly Spheres.* Translated by Christine M. Grimm. Twin Lakes, WI: Arcana Publishing, 2000.

Shakespeare, William. 1958. *Tragedies.* Edited by Peter Alexander. London: William Collins Son & Company.

The Shepherd of Hermas. (1926) 2009. In *The Lost Books of the Bible: Being All the Gospels, Epistles, and Other Pieces Now Extant.* New York: Alpha House. Revised by John Bruno Hare. Internet Sacred Text Archive. http://www. sacred-texts.com/bib/lbob/lbob26.htm.

Skinner, Stephen, and David Rankine. 2004. *Practical Angel Magic of Dr. John Dee's Enochian Tables.* Singapore: Golden Hoard Press.

Steiner, Rudolf. 1994. *The Archangel Michael: His Mission and Ours.* Hudson, NY: Anthroposophic Press.

Steinsaltz, Adin. 1989. *The Talmud: The Steinhaltz Edition,* Vol. 1: *Tractate Bava Metzia, Part One.* New York: Random House.

Schneible, Ann. 2014. "Be Like Children—Believe in Your Guardian Angel, Pope Says." *Catholic News Agency,* October 4. http://www.catholicnewsagency.com/news/ be-like-children-believe-in-your-guardian-angel-pope-says-55343/.

Swedenborg, Emanuel. 1976. *Heaven and Hell.* Translated by George F. Dole. New York: Pillar Books.

The Sibylline Oracles. 1899. Translated by Milton S. Terry. New York: Eaton and Mains.

Tyson, Donald. 1997. *Enochian Magic for Beginners: The Original System of Angel Magic.* St. Paul, MN: Llewellyn Publications.

Thompson, Francis. 1893. "Ex Ore Infantium." *Merry England.* May.

Webber, Bill. 2009. "The Angels of Martin Luther King, Jr." Beliefnet, January. http://www.beliefnet.com/inspiration/angels/2009/01/angels-of-martin-luther-king-jr.aspx.

Webster, Richard. 1998. *Spirit Guides & Angel Guardians: Contact Your Invisible Helpers.* St. Paul, MN: Llewellyn Publications.

———. 2004. *Michael: Communicating with the Archangel for Guidance & Protection.* St. Paul, MN: Llewellyn Publications.

———. 2005. *Gabriel: Communicating with the Archangel for Inspiration & Reconciliation.* St. Paul, MN: Llewellyn Publications.

———. 2005. *Raphael: Communicating with the Archangel for Healing & Creativity.* St. Paul, MN: Llewellyn Publications.

———. 2005. *Uriel: Communicating with the Archangel for Transformation & Tranquility.* Woodbury, MN: Llewellyn Publications, 2005.

———. 2007. *Praying with Angels*. Woodbury, MN: Llewellyn Publications.

———. 2009. *Encyclopedia of Angels*. Woodbury, MN: Llewellyn Publications.

———. 2016. *Rituals for Beginners: Simple Ways to Connect to Your Spiritual Side*. Woodbury, MN: Llewellyn Publications.

Wilson, Peter Lamborn. 1980. *Angels: Messengers of the Gods*. London: Thames and Hudson.

Von Hochheim, Eckhart. 1998. "Sermon Nine." Featured in *The Reading and Preaching of the Scriptures in the Worship of the Christian Church* by Hughes Oliphant Old. Vol. 3, *The Medieval Church*. Grand Rapids, MI: Wm. B. Eerdmans Publishing Company.

To Write to the Author

If you wish to contact the author or would like more information about this book, please write to the author in care of Llewellyn Worldwide Ltd., and we will forward your request. Both the author and publisher appreciate hearing from you and learning of your enjoyment of this book and how it has helped you. Llewellyn Worldwide Ltd. cannot guarantee that every letter written to the author can be answered, but all will be forwarded. Please write to:

Richard Webster
℅ Llewellyn Worldwide
2143 Wooddale Drive
Woodbury, MN 55125-2989

Please enclose a self-addressed stamped envelope for reply, or $1.00 to cover costs. If outside the USA, enclose an international postal reply coupon.

ENCYCLOPEDIA
of
ANGELS

RICHARD
WEBSTER

Encyclopedia of Angels
RICHARD WEBSTER

Angels lend comfort and strength in times of difficulty, bring our lofty goals down to earth, and set our spirits soaring toward the divine. No matter what spiritual path you travel, the angels are there to offer guidance and inspiration along the way.

International best-selling author and angel expert Richard Webster presents this alphabetically-arranged book of angels, a collection of over 500, hailing from diverse traditions, cultures, and belief systems all over the world. A snapshot of each angel's traits, abilities, and specialties illustrates the myriad ways in which these heavenly helpers can deepen your spiritual practice and enrich your life.

- Discover the roles of angels in various spiritual texts and religions throughout history
- Meet your guardian angel, the archangels, the angel presiding over your astrological sign, and more
- Learn the best methods, most propitious times, and just exactly how to communicate with each angel

You hold in your hands the ultimate resource for getting in touch with the divine. Open your heart to the miraculous powers of the angels, and fill your life with the peace, encouragement, and blessings that you've always wanted.

978-0-7387-1462-2, 264 pp., 6 x 9   **$16.99**
